Bernard Jones And The Temple Of Mammon

The continuing diary of a cantankerous investor

by Nick Louth

Harriman House Ltd
3A Penns Road
Petersfield
Hampshire
GU32 2EW

Tel: +44 (0)1730 233870
Fax: +44(0)1730 233880
Email: enquiries@harriman-house.com
Website: www.harriman-house.com

First published in Great Britain in 2007 by Harriman House Ltd.
Ludensian Books
Copyright © Nick Louth

www.nicklouth.com

www.bernardjones.co.uk

ISBN 978-0-9554939-1-1

British Library Cataloguing in Publication Data
A CIP catalogue record for this book can be obtained from the British Library

Printed and bound by Biddles Ltd, Kings Lynn, Norfolk.

"The funniest and most realistic book ever written about investment."

– *Investors Chronicle*

Praise For Funny Money

"In Bernard Jones, Nick Louth has produced an anti-hero for our financial age. Whether it is fighting his way to a secure retirement, jousting with the council over wheelie bins or feuding with his wife over his fondness for cakes and biscuits, Bernard Jones goes into battle on behalf of us all."

Matthew Vincent, Editor, *Investors Chronicle*

"Nick Louth delightfully and painfully accurately brings to life the travails of the amateur investor as he tries to make his pension stretch that little bit further. Nick's wry humour and witty focus on human relationships and frailties is a must read and requires no knowledge of finance to enjoy."

Ashley Seager, *The Guardian*

"Just as chick-lit heroine Bridget Jones struggles with men, retired anti-hero Bernard Jones is bemused by the trials and tribulations of investing. Anyone who is a member of an investment club will instantly recognise the characters in this clever, well crafted and highly amusing book."

Brian Durrant, Investment Director, The Fleet Street Letter

"Bernard Jones, tried by life, marriage, family, friends and neighbours as much as by investment is a must-read. He's on the way to becoming a minor classic."

Chris Crowcroft, *Investors Chronicle* reader

"I have enjoyed reading Bernard Jones Diary as he attempts to enjoy retirement with a mixture of cunning and (not too much) knowledge. I wish him well."

Eric Cox, *Investors Chronicle* reader

"It's so easy to identify with Bernard Jones and the situations he describes. I almost feel I know him as a friend. His diary is the first page I turn to in the magazine. It is always topical and hugely entertaining."

Leonard Spark, *Investors Chronicle* reader

"Small time investor Bernard Jones juggles with middle age, a wife, a grown up family, an elderly mother, foul neighbours and investments. His only pleasures are his indulgence in secretive sweet treats and a Hornby train set. Life shifts up a gear when a pretty au pair arrives next door."

Joe Vella, *Investors Chronicle* reader

"Bernard and I are soul mates...We share the same hopeless investing traits being driven by misty eyed emotion, alcohol and a love of chocolate rather than the cold logical appraisal of information so beloved by the professionals."

Gordon Gray, New Zealand, *Investors Chronicle* reader

"I have found myself laughing out loud and occasionally in giggles!"

Mark Hobhouse, *Investors Chronicle* reader

"A must read for the private investor...Share the highs and lows of life with Bernard as he battles the twin impostors of triumph and despair (not in equal measure unfortunately)."

Tony Watson, *Investors Chronicle* reader

"Don't miss Bernard's diary, it will brighten your day. This addictive column is so true to life."

Paul Hunt, *Investors Chronicle* reader

About The Author

Nick Louth is a financial journalist, author and investment commentator. He has regular columns in the *Financial Times*, the *Investors Chronicle* and on the MSN Money website.

His first book, an investment guide called *Multiply your Money*, was published by McGraw Hill in November 2001. *Funny Money: The (Investment) Diary of Bernard Jones* followed in February 2007, and a novel, *Bite*, in October 2007.

Nick Louth is married and lives in rural Lincolnshire.

For Louise

No actuaries, accountants or stockbrokers were harmed
during the writing or production of this book.

Foreword

Welcome to the second collection of the Bernard Jones investment diaries. Bernard Jones originally began as a one-off feature idea for the *Investors Chronicle* for the Christmas edition of 2005. The plan, to leaven the magazine's heavier fare of share tips and analysis with some light-hearted comic fiction, worked so well that editor Matthew Vincent asked me to revive Bernard as a weekly and topical column for the magazine.

This book is more than a collection of previously published columns. As with the previous volume, a good third of the book is new and unpublished material.

The first volume of the diaries, *Funny Money*, was published in February 2007 by Ludensian Books.

Those who want to follow Bernard's adventures week-by-week will find a subscriber offer to the *Investors Chronicle* in this book.

There is much more background information on Bernard Jones and the other characters at the website www.bernardjones.co.uk and on the *Investors Chronicle's* own site www.investorschronicle.co.uk.

Nick Louth

November 2007

Introduction

Retired civil servant Bernard Jones, now heading towards his 64th birthday, is not finding life gets any easier. Making money through investing remains as elusive as ever, though his wife Eunice finds no trouble spending it. Hell's Bells, the share club started at the Ring o'Bells pub by a coterie of dubious acquaintances, seems to be a better forum for gawping at barmaids and consuming pork scratchings than it is for the elevated debate over price earnings ratios and dividend yields. Bernard seeks investment club solace in the company of septuagenarian former navy officer Harry Staines, perpetual loser Martin Gale and self-made convenience store tycoon K.P. Sharma. Joining them at beer-ringed tables and tacky carpets are the eyebrow and lip-pierced Goth barmaid Chantelle, whose investment acumen comes from being a scrap dealer's daughter, and the quiet cigarette king Mike Delaney. The arrival of hyper-efficient ex-City professional Cynthia Valkenberg is not quite the coincidence that it appears.

Eunice, ever the killjoy, is determined that Bernard's lifespan will exceed his ability to finance it, and uses every ounce of feminine guile to track down every cholesterol-rich snack, biscuit and cake that Bernard can conceal. While Bernard is allowed to eat at elevenses, Eunice is most likely to switch his chosen comestible for an obscure tropical fruit noted for its balance of selenium and zinc.

Bernard's 90-year-old mother remains the scourge of his dreams of inheritance. By turns confused, lucid and vindictive, dotty Dot enrages Bernard through her determination to keep all her valuable financial eggs in one highly vulnerable basket. She has a huge £600,000 shareholding in BAe Systems, courtesy of her long-departed husband, but despite the controversy over the firm's past activities in Saudi Arabia, she refuses to countenance spreading this wealth over a wider range of shares, and moves deftly to block all Bernard's attempts to change her mind.

Bernard's grandson Digby, an irritant since infancy, hasn't changed his spots since reaching eight. With the dubious distinction of being expelled from a playgroup at the age of two, for biting a little girl's ear, Digby (who shares a birthday with Pol Pot) has now turned into a more calculatedly malevolent force in Bernard's life. One day he changes all the settings on his grandfather's PC to tiny and illegible fonts in canary yellow, another time he cunningly offers a confectionery-starved Bernard some illicit biscuits with all the casual aplomb of a playground drug dealer. No wonder Bernard still quietly refers to Digby as The Antichrist, though his parents, Bernard's schoolteacher son Brian and his wife Janet, do not seem to see the evil that lies beneath.

However, it is during a long weekend in the north that Bernard finally sees the light. At the Temple of Mammon, a bluff Yorkshireman gives Bernard and the other male members of the share club a piece of advice that is both sage and down-to-earth. The lessons learned on this trip, some sternly administered, are not complete until Bernard's encounter with the formidable Mistress Sadie.

Finally though, Bernard does find out where his heart lies. He discovers that his first and dearest love, Amelia Wrigley, is actually back in the country almost fifty years since their last encounter. In 1961, at aged eighteen, Bernard carved 'B.J. loves A.W.' on a pear tree in the orchard at Old Dorringsfield. That orchard latterly became the site of a planning application by Celandine Homes, run by the notorious local villains Greg and Barry Harmsworth. Thanks to Bernard's intervention, the Harmsworths have a grudge against him. That, however, is not uppermost in his mind as he goes to make an assignation with Amelia.

Acknowledgements

I should like to thank all those who helped me in the research for this book. While the characters and storyline are fictional, much of the investment background against which they develop is factual.

Without the help and assistance of the *Investors Chronicle*, particularly Matthew Vincent, Rosie Carr and Erica Morgan, this book would not have been possible. David Benson at DAB Graphics was patient with my many demands. Myles Hunt and his colleagues at Harriman House have been continually supportive throughout the ups and downs of the process of turning Bernard Jones from a magazine column into a book.

Finally, and as always, I should like to thank my wife Louise for her support and encouragement. Let me add once again, for those who suspect some autobiographical notes in these diaries, that not only I am nothing at all like Bernard, she is nothing like Eunice.

Chapter One

Mr Twenty Per Cent

New Year's Eve: Thompson Twinge

Having lost six per cent in 2006, Hell's Bells may be one of the more ramshackle share clubs in terms of performance, but I like to think we get our dividends in fun. Our New Year's party at the Ring o'Bells went with a swing, partly because most of us had been let off the family leash for the evening. However, the one 'other half' who did attend was Mrs Sharma, looking resplendent in a glittering green sari and half moon specs. As the pub couldn't get kitchen staff, she supplied most of the food, including the notorious thermonuclear samosas. However the tandoori lamb was divine, and the fish madras with lime quite exquisite. Still, such fare needs plenty of lubrication and after three pints of hand-pulled Spitfire I head off on a rather wobbly sortie to the toilet. Lurching through the door, I see it's been refurbished in lime green (do I detect Chantelle's tastes here?) The moment I reach my destination, there is a hiss and something that smells like Tom Jones's aftershave is squirted about me. Looking up I see the skull-like 'fragrance disperser' and the dread emblem of Rentokil Initial. Similarly emblazoned is the (empty) soap dispenser and the (non-working) hand-dryer.

Rentokil was one of my first and worst share forays, as I fell under the spell of one Clive (now Sir Clive) Thompson, a.k.a. Mr Twenty Percent. I bought in the middle of 1998 at about 400p when the firm could do no wrong, spilling out profits faster than paper towels from a badly fitted dispenser. Soon however, growth came as reluctantly as sheets of toilet paper from those big metal drums which are designed to stop the theft of the roll, and on which I once cut my knuckles at Gatwick Airport. I eventually sold at 225p, having missed the brief chance to sell at 475p in the 2000 bubble. The collapse of Sir Clive's low income savers' firm Farepak last year brought back distasteful memories.

Now the final Thompson challenge. A new washbasin has replaced the cracked old thing which always leaked. However, its shiny minimalist taps (labelled F and C: Did the pub try to save money by ordering surplus Congolese or Paraguayan versions?) have no obvious mode of operation. Nothing to twist. No foot pedal. I press tap C. Absolutely rigid. I try waving my hands in front in case they are cunningly infrared operated, which in the mirror makes me a Tommy Copper impersonator (just like that). But still nothing. At this moment Harry Staines lurches in, cannons off two walls and into the cubicle, whose door he leaves open as he does his Victoria Falls impersonation.

"Do you know how these work, Harry?"

"I never trust a tap," he says enigmatically as he strides out to join the great unwashed.

Finally, I press the top of the other tap. Instantly a ferocious spray of freezing water (so that's what the F stands for) hits me at trouser height. After some Anglo-Saxon vocal exercises, I find there is absolutely nothing, neither towel, curtain nor sheet of toilet paper in this Rentokil khazi to dry out these embarrassing dark patches. Furtively, I emerge in search of beer towels and run straight into Mrs Sharma, who takes one trouser-ward glance and flees. Oh God! I think Sir Clive has cursed me.

Wednesday 3ʳᵈ January 2007: Vintage Misery

Edgington dinner party on Saturday. Peter's scribbled message on the invitation said "celebrating a vintage year in 2006". He's bound to gloat about his share-picking performance. I find this too depressing for words.

 Elevenses: Eunice and I had a huge row about cholesterol and diet over Christmas, culminating in her flouncing off to the spare room. Three days of bliss, safe from snoring and dreaded hippopotamus manoeuvres. However, the final compromise forced on me is to give up the Hornby drawer key, though I can still (for now) eat what I like.

 Close of play: Down £270, second loss in a row. I thought January was supposed to be a good month.

Thursday 4ᵗʰ January: Share Checkers Anonymous

After a first day frenzy, the market seems to have gone soggy. However, I'm going to try to make a New Year's resolution of only checking share prices three times a day. Once at the open, once at elevenses, and once at close of play. That's really perfectly adequate. Yet I have to admit the lure of that little screen portfolio tool is very strong. While I'm trying to research what I should buy this year by doing some fundamental research, I have developed this crackhead's habit of doing a sneaky click to see if Domino's Pizza or BAe have added 1p or lost 1p in the last ten minutes. Who cares, Bernard? You are in for years not weeks, yet here we go again. Click. BAe up 2p.

Elevenses: Now, here's a curious thing. Came to eat the last eccles cake from drawer and found a small self-adhesive red dot on it. What on earth does this mean?

Sunday 7ᵗʰ January: Perfect Peter Entertains

The Edgington dinner party last night saw Peter at his most nauseating. While Geraldine showed Eunice her collection of Edwardian jewellery, Peter walked me through his successes for 2006, most of which seem to have soared *and* pay big dividends: Scottish & Southern Electricity, Viridian, Irish building products firm Kingspan, HBOS, Northern Rock, and Persimmon. Had he lost money on anything at all, I wondered?

"Almost," he said. "I made very little when I sold BG Group. However, it was clear that wholesale gas prices were going down from about August, so I would have lost out had I waited."

How awful for him. To *nearly* lose money.

 Elevenses: A plain chocolate Bounty. As I opened it, I saw it had been labelled with an orange stick-on dot. What can this mean?

Monday 8ᵗʰ January: The Quatermass Experiment

Peter's successes all seemed to come in value stocks, the flavour of the year in 2006. Surely this can hardly continue when even dull old electricity firms rise by 50 per cent in a year. Also read a piece of research from the U.S. which said that the shares covered by the fewest analysts did best. Now we know just how overpaid those chinless City wonders are. When Goldman Sachs initiates coverage we should probably sell.

 Elevenses: A curious green finned fruit-like object has materialised in the Hornby drawer. There's no obvious fuse or explosive charge, but it does sport a green adhesive dot. I leave Prescott, Jemima's suede pig, to guard it while I seek enlightenment from on high.

"It's a star fruit, Bernard. You must have seen them," Eunice said.

"It's more like something Dr Quatermass dreamt up on an off-day," I retorted. "What am I supposed to do with it?"

"Eat it in slices. It's full of vitamin C. That's why I gave it a green light."

"Green light. Ah! Is that what those silly dots are all about?"

"They're not silly, that's the government traffic light scheme to label food according to how healthy it is."

"I know, but if the supermarkets don't want it, why should you impose it within the household?"

"Supermarkets don't want it for obvious reasons. They want people to buy fatty foods because they are more profitable."

"Supermarkets don't reveal their profit margin by product. It's a closely guarded secret. Don't tell me you've been doing some share research of your own?"

"Don't be facetious, Bernard. It's perfectly obvious. Fresh foods are an open book. An apple, a parsnip or a carrot has a value the shopper can relate to. They couldn't charge us £1 each because we'd know from common sense it's too much. Yet who knows what arcane processes go into making a packet of Hula Hoops, a sausage or one of your precious eccles cakes? The truth is that we think we know the right price, yet the cost of ingredients is far less than we suspect because of cheap sweeteners and industrial hydrogenated fats."

"You're ignoring the fact that supermarkets don't make their own products," I said.

"Of course. They buy them in cheaply. Anyway, I really don't want all that rubbish clogging up your arteries. That is why I have started labelling your elevenses."

Eunice oversees me as I eat the thing. It has a curious waxy texture and is mildly sweet, but I can't escape the worry that I'll swell up like the Elephant Man and be sent to intensive care.

Tuesday 9th January: Global Warbling

Rank, my pick for the share club, has continued to drift since news of the poor price gained for selling Hard Rock Café to the Seminoles. Forty years ago, Red Indians were being slaughtered on screen by John Wayne and co. Now, as Native Americans, they are raking in gambling money and buying up international restaurant chains. Still, I read that other potential bidders were shut out and are threatening to Sioux.

 Elevenses: A packet of crushed Hula Hoops from the bargain bin at Kwik Save. 11p!

Radio 4 interviewed the obscenely youthful environment minister, David Millipede. So articulate, but with 1,000 to choose from he's bound to put a foot in it sooner or later. He was responding to the PM being taken to task for flying abroad on holiday. Well, you can hardly imagine him sitting on the beach at Clacton with a knotted hankie on his head, can you? I'm no fan (whether sustainably powered or not) of Blair but I'm sure he's on target to make government travel carbon neutral. The obvious plan is to pipe the by-products of combustion deep into cavernous and otherwise unusable storage spaces, such as John Prescott. The Germans are already using Helmut Kohl mines, so we have to keep up.

Actually, I'm heartily sick of this tosh about global warming. I can recall that in the 1980s we were supposed to freeze to death because of a nuclear winter, and now we're all going to drown as sea levels rise. Like the Millennium Bug it probably won't happen. But even so, am I missing an investment opportunity?

Tuesday 9th January (later): Toyboy Tales

9pm. Eunice out with Irmgard when phone rings. Turns out to be Angharad, former head girl, life class model and chief sorceress of St Celia's old girls' coven. As always, she catches me off balance.

"How are your shares, Bernard?"

"Oh, they're fine."

"Being such a sophisticated operator, I expect you have taken full advantage of REITs," she cooed.

"Well, I'm certainly looking into that whole area."

"Only looking? That's a bit late, surely. Buy on the rumour sell on the fact, that's what Larry and I do. I think real estate has had its best moment in the run up to this news."

She then brags shamelessly about her new husband. Larry is a director of Morgan Stanley, a superb yachtsman and an international equestrian. Angharad, whose appetites make Kimberly Quinn look like a nun, has already worn out and divested two husbands, each a few years younger than herself. This one is apparently eight years her junior. Eunice, excited and horrified in equal measure by this carry-on, will be expecting me to remember every detail. The point of the call, though, is the death of one of the old girls, Helena. This being the St Celia's crew, it wasn't something typical for a fiftyish dame, such as cancer or even a car crash, but a snowboarding tragedy in Klosters.

"The funeral's in your neck of the woods, on Friday. Hope you can be there too. There's a friend of mine I'd like you to meet. She might like to join your share club."

Wednesday 10th January: Thinking Outside The Wine Box

Not doing too well on my resolution of cutting down on share checking. Bovis moved about quite a bit after its trading statement yesterday. Must have looked at the price fifteen times already.

Hm. Bovis down 10p.

3pm. First 2007 share club meeting at the Ring o'Bells, and there are a few changes. Harry Staines has a moustache, K.P. Sharma has a new suit, and Mike Delaney is sporting a lemon-coloured pullover. Sadly, this Christmas sartorial spruce-up, sponsored by long-suffering wife Sheila, has already come to naught. The sweater is already dusted with cigarette ash and one sleeve is unravelling. Martin Gale, struggling under his IVA, lets slip that he has found alternative investments which the insolvency bods can't detect. We wait for the punch line.

"I'm investing in wine."

"But that costs thousands," K.P. Sharma splutters.

"Aha! Not necessarily."

"But what about the IVA?" I ask. "Won't they want their cut?"

"It's going on the Tesco bill like anything else. I'm really just siphoning off cash from the housekeeping."

"Can you get the top chateaux you need there?" I ask.

"I'm not going for top chateaux. I'm laying down Bulgarian wines. It's a kind of contrarian move, see. No-one thinks anything of Bulgarian wine at the moment, but now they've joined the EU there will be loads of French money outsourcing production to cheaper places. What I've got in my garage are like the AIM stocks of the wine world. And at £1.89 a bottle!"

However dubious the profit prospects, you have to admire his originality.

Chapter Two

Alternative Investment

Thursday 11th January: Mum On The Blink

6.50am. Dot phones up saying her TV's gone on the blink.

"What are you watching at this time of day?" I ask blearily.

"Question Time with Robin Day."

Good grief, the BBC is digging even deeper for overnight repeats than I had feared. "What's wrong with it?" I ask her.

"It's all fuzzy. I can't hear what they're saying."

"The picture's fuzzy or the sound? Try changing channel."

I hear a few bangs. "Use the remote, Mum. They don't have dials any more!" I yell.

"It's no good Bernard, it's broken. Can you call the man from Radio Rentals?"

"It's from Comet, Mum. You didn't rent it. Find the service agreement."

"Ooh, I don't have one of those." After a few minutes of yes-you-dos and no-I-don'ts I realise I shall have to go round.

11am. The moment I get there I realise there is nothing wrong with the TV at all. The problem is with the viewer. Dot is wearing a pair of horn-rimmed glasses that look vaguely familiar.

"Those aren't your glasses are they, Mum?"

"No, they're Geoffrey's, I found them in the utility room. I've lost mine." That, of course, is why the picture was fuzzy, and why my 90-minute journey has once again been wasted. While searching for her specs, I mention that later today I shall sell the first of her BAe shares, now that she has given me permission.

"No you won't. I never gave you permission."

Oh God, how long do I have to be tortured with this?

Friday 12th January: Not-so-free Kick

David Beckham is joining the Philip Anschutz media circus for the staggering sum of $250m in an attempt to turn soccer into a mainstream sport in the U.S. I'm no fan of the ugly game, but I do recall Phil's previous rodeo pal, John Prescott, was only able to bend things like Beckham by sitting on them.

Elevenses: Had smuggled into the Hornby drawer a double pack of mince pies (special post-Christmas buy-one-get-one-free offer). Carefully put them in the box in which the double O heavy lift crane had come, as camouflage against wandering health gestapo. Despite this, each and every pie has been marked with a red stick-on dot.

3.30pm. Relying on Eunice's map-reading skills, we were late for Helena's funeral. Finally, we tramped up to a crumbling gothic church in a howling gale. The churchyard was overshadowed by creaking sycamores and echoed to the cawing of rooks. St Cecilia's old girls had turned out in black-clad force and were silhouetted against the fading sun like a Scottish Widows reunion. While Eunice gushed apologies, Angharad introduced me to the others in best head girl manner.

"Now this is Cynthia Valkenberg," Angharad said. "She's just moved into the Manor House at Old Dorringsfield and is interested in your share club."

Cynthia was a tall and angular redhead in her late thirties with designer specs and a slight transatlantic twang. I remarked on what a wonderful building the manor was, and then immediately put my foot in it.

"So what does your other half do to afford a magnificent pile like that?" I asked.

"Excuse me?"

"Is he a City type then, or was it property?" I said, hurtling further down the causeway of conversational catastrophe.

"What makes you think I didn't buy it myself?"

"Oh. My goodness, you have done well," I added, hoping that a bijou compliment would allow me to escape.

"Wouldn't you say that's just a little patronising, Mr Jones?"

In the end I just blabbed my apologies, which were accepted. Just when matters had recovered I finished off with a little small talk:

"So what part of the States are you from, then?"

"No part, as it happens. I'm a Canadian."

Oh God! Perhaps they should just have buried me, not Helena.

Monday 15th January: Full Marks For Trying

Marks & Spencer, bane of my brief short-selling career, has now announced it is to go carbon neutral, presumably in a bid to grab the right-on middle-aged female customer from the clammy embrace of John Lewis and Waitrose. All the plastic packaging is now going to be recycled into clothing, so presumably it's back to the 1970s with acrylic golfing pullovers, crimpelene kaftans, nylon housecoats that whistle while you walk, and terylene socks that shrink to the size of a hamster's condom after the first wash. Not sure how this will save the planet, unless it makes everyone too embarrassed to leave home.

Elevenses: Trying to throw Eunice off the scent, bought a family pack of Kellogg's Nutri-Grain bars (raspberry flavour). Appear healthy, but having read the label I knew better.

It's laced with sugar, honey, dextrose and something called 'high fructose corn syrup'. Mistake. First bite reveals it is too sickly even for me. That's £2.70 wasted.

Close of play: Tanfield going great guns! Up 10 per cent in one day to 68p, which makes the rest of the portfolio look like it's standing still. Actually, the rest of the portfolio is standing still. So is the whole market.

Tuesday 16ᵗʰ January: BP Hammered

Viciously hard-hitting report on BP's safety record from the U.S. I'm so glad I never bought the shares. Recall that Peter Edgington did. Looking back through the diary see that he says he paid 640p for them in October 2005. As they are now around 530p, can't see how he can claim not to have lost money on anything last year. Will have to tackle him about this. If he's been fibbing that would be very interesting.

Elevenses: Eunice dragged me out clothes shopping, so had to make do with a cuppa in the café by Waitrose. Her driving is getting very bad. I noticed a largish dent in the middle of the Clio's back bumper, which to me had 'supermarket concrete post' written all over it. Then, as so very often, Eunice got in the wrong side for the petrol at the filling station, and then looked baffled when the filler cap wasn't on the side by the pump. When she finally clambered back in, having wrestled with the pump and got dirty hands, she snarled that cars were obviously designed by men. I asked why.

"Obviously, Bernard, if they were designed by a woman there would be a fuel cap on each side."

"That's absurd."

"Why? They do it with headlamps, don't they?"

Wednesday 17th January: Not For Beginners

Arrived late at the share club meeting. Harry Staines, now in possession of an incipient ponytail, catches my attention at the bar of the Ring o'Bells before I go through to the back room.

"There's a tall speccy ginger bint in there says she's waiting for you. Is she your bit on the side?"

Baffled by this acerbic description, I walk in to see Cynthia Valkenberg, perched on a threadbare bar stool and nursing a Campari. In defiance of Ring o'Bells norms she's wearing a formal trouser suit and patent leather shoes. Martin Gale, K.P. Sharma and Mike Delaney are sitting in apparent shock with their backs toward the far wall. I too am amazed because after the exchanges at the funeral I thought she'd never want to clap eyes on me again.

"Quite a place, isn't it?" Cynthia says, taking in the dinghy curtains, sticky carpets and empty crisp packets stuffed in the ashtrays. "So are you interested in having a female member?"

"We're an equal opportunity outfit, darling," says Harry, walking in with a pint in each hand. "We'll happily teach you the ins and outs of investing."

Cynthia winces slightly, and after adjusting her glasses asks some intelligent questions about subscription levels, voting and so on. K.P. Sharma starts to explain the rules, and shows her a print out of our portfolio. At this she chuckles. "Three stocks, is that it?"

"We've only been going a year or so," says Martin defensively.

"Look. I don't mean to be funny, but I've got £100,000 in a current account that needs investing and more elsewhere, but if you are just a bunch of amateurs there's no point in me staying."

The idea of a hundred grand to play with starts to sink in. K.P.

Sharma turned to us and notes this would mean we could build a real portfolio.

"So come on guys," she says. "Are we gonna get rich together or not?" The answer is a resounding 'yes'. Cynthia even buys a round.

Thursday 18ᵗʰ January: £8m Goody Bag

6pm. Severe gales. Eunice glued to TV in the conservatory watching Irmgard's tapes of each dreary missed episode of *Celebrity Big Brother*. "Bernard, you should see this. There's a very pretty Indian girl."

"I'd rather watch the fire go out," I reply as I paint the hat on a double O gauge ticket collector. "You know, when I was a boy I used to drop beetles and ants into a jar and shake them to see if they'd fight. This programme is nothing more than a shaking a jar of dim footballers, addled dental assistants, has-been actors and sundry other fluff to see who says 'boo' to whom."

"Oh, don't be such a snob."

"I'm sorry, but in my opinion Channel Four has just stuffed a camera up society's backside and everyone seems surprised the result is flatulent nonsense."

Just then a huge gust sent the O'Riordan's trampoline flying over the hedge and smack into the back of the conservatory, shearing off one of the super-expensive gold effect patio door handles. Great. That adds to the £137.25 I lost in the markets today.

Actually, *Big Brother* isn't entirely dull as an Internet search reveals. Shilpa Shetty was paid £360,000, far more than any other contestant, to brighten up proceedings. However this wealth pales into insignificance compared with Jade Goody's £8m goody bag, which includes earnings promoting a perfume (called Ming, if I remember rightly) and the £1bn fortune that 47-year-old *Big Brother* founder John de Mol has built from the show's format. For unlikely money-spinners, BB ranks alongside Perrier (getting people to buy water when it's free from the tap), texting (cumbersome oaf-to-oaf messaging whr spelng dnt mttr), changing rooms (watching other people's paint dry) and Paul Daniels (need I say more?)

Saturday 20th January: Bin Unladen

7.20am. Bang at front of house. Daphne Hanson-Hart has reversed into our gatepost for the fourth time in two years. However, this time she has knocked over our green waste bin too, spreading potato peelings and other goo far and wide.

"Sorry Bernard," she says, as I emerge. "I forgot I wasn't in the mini."

How this explains the collision, I'm not sure. "Don't worry. I know how you feel about wheelie bins. If you'd aimed a foot to the right you could have knocked over the recycling and household waste bins too." I notice the back of hubby's BMW is looking as careworn these days as Keith Richards' face.

On return to the den I scan through a copy of Chronic Investor, when what should I see but a recommendation for a Greek wheelie bin maker. Helesi already has a six per cent share of the European market and is growing fast, yet the P/E ratio is only nine. It might not be the most exciting company going, but enraging Daphne has got to be worth something.

Chapter Three
Gales Of Fortune

Sunday 21st January: Beach Boys

Peaceful solitary breakfast of scrambled eggs and bacon while reading the *Telegraph*. Take quiet satisfaction from the huge MoD training order won by QinetiQ, which has added 20p to the shares in the last few days. Still, if a bunch of ex-MoD staff cannot chivvy work out of their old mates, the sales team should be shot. My reverie is broken by animated squeals from the conservatory. Eunice is watching TV and pointing animatedly at the screen. It's apparently a new reality programme, where contestants race to scavenge the contents of shipping containers washed up on a beach in Devon. Eunice, mouth crammed with toast, is unable to explain her excitement until we get another view of the beach and two men prying a BMW motorcycle from its packaging and pushing it up the shingle.

My God! It's Harry Staines and Martin Gale. The share club's two greatest eccentrics have taken the philosophy of alternative investments to a new level. Asked by the interviewer about the legality of their salvage operation, Harry says that he is only there to help protect a pristine marine environment. "This crankcase is full of oil which could damage crabs and other creatures," he says, adding, "I've given up my Sunday to help prevent another Torrey Canyon disaster." He and Martin then push the bike into the back of a transit van and drive off.

Tuesday 23rd January: Battleaxe Bullying

10.45am. Am happily watching the FTSE move up and down, when Eunice marches into the den, catching me with a mini roll in hand. "Don't forget the doctor's appointment today," she says, removing the offending item from my grasp.

"What appointment?"

"About your blood test."

"What blood test? I haven't had one."

"No, but you will."

Half an hour later we're sitting in the office of the dreaded Dr Ross, the Ann Widdecombe lookalike with the interfering fingers.

"How's the prostate today, Mr Jones?" she asks brightly.

"In tip-top condition and not in need of any manual fine tuning," I answer.

"Bernard," Eunice interjects. "You're still getting up two or three times a night."

This is duly noted. "And how are you doing on improving your diet?" Dr Ross asks as she starts scribbling. "Are you getting five portions of fruit and vegetables a day? And cutting out the sugar?"

As I answer yes, I notice Eunice rummaging in her bag. Along the desk she lays out seven foil jam and lemon tart containers, four Bounty wrappers, a Kellogg's Nutri-Grain packet, a Cadbury's Mini Roll wrapper and a receipt for a bumper Christmas box of eccles cakes. As the quack looks up, Eunice gestures to the packaging. "This is evidence I retrieved from the bin, just in the last three weeks. It's a sustained and secretive habit of high fat, high sugar rubbish. I'm sorry to say that my husband is in denial."

So, my blood is duly and painfully extracted and I'm warned by the white-coated battleaxe that should the results again show high cholesterol, a 'diet regime' will have to be implemented.

Close of play: Up £16.50. Tanfield still going great guns! Realise that I've only a few days to get Eunice an anniversary present. After 40 years penile servitude, I think I've earned a nice gift myself. Seem to remember the great train robbers got a shorter sentence and were let out halfway.

Wednesday 24th January: Mezzanine Finance

Saw Peter Edgington in town. Asked him about the BP shares he bought in October 2005, and whether he still had them. He then claimed that he had never repurchased them after his usual Sell-in-May-and-Go-Away exercise in 2006, which he executed at 680p for a profit of 40p a share. Is his judgement really this uncanny? I do find it hard to believe. Then he tells me that the BP proceeds are being ploughed into an extension for his French holiday home. He just happens to have the architect's plans with him, showing a whole new floor at the back of the house, between ground and first floor levels, from which guests will be able to see the Saint-Émilion wine harvest. Do I care? Yes, I'm greener than Jonathan Porritt's allotment.

Elevenses: My last mini rolls have been swiped from the Hornby drawer. Fuming. Eunice out, so no-one to have row with. Fridge booby-trapped with celeriac, jerusalem artichokes and red chard. Cupboards devoid of all biscuits and cakes, bar a dusty packet of glace cherries. Relief turns out to be short-lived, as these have been petrified into vermilion marbles. Best before Jan 1997, says the packet, so I suck 'em like gobstoppers.

Thursday 25th January: Mineral Stakes

Am just off to get Eunice an anniversary present. I asked her what she would like and she said, "Well, it IS our ruby wedding anniversary."

"No, I think forty is cubic zirconium," I responded, earning myself a withering glance.

Friday 26ᵗʰ January: Diversification Attempt

A single inch of snow once again maims Britain's motorway network. Crawl round to Isleworth for lunch with Dot at the local Baker's Oven. Following the new strategy I am attempting to charm her into letting me sell the bulk of her BAe Systems shares, even letting her choose this gastronomica geriatrica to eat at. Feel I must make progress before world trade bodies start their own fraud investigations into Al Yamamah kickbacks, which could kibosh the shares. Discussion gets off to a poor start.

"So, Mum, I really think you should let me sell some of those shares and spread them across lots of other companies."

"Why's that?" she says, her face moustached with flecks of Gregg's highly profitable sausage roll.

"Like I've said, there is a risk that if you have all your financial eggs in one basket, they could get broken."

"Is it a chicken company then, Bernard? You said it made Spitfires."

"No I DIDN'T. I said it made jet fighters. Plus warships, missiles, bullets and shells."

"Eggshells?"

"NO! For God's sake, Mum! Forget eggs, for a minute, would you?"

"Well you brought them up."

"I didn't. It was a metaphor..."

"You never liked them even when you were a toddler as I recall. Boiled was alright, but you could never managed scrambled because it reminded you of sick."

"Please, for pity's sake…" At this point my forehead was resting on the table.

"Alright, Bernard alright," she smiled, patting my shoulder. "I'll let you have your way."

Slowly I raise my head, not daring to believe it. Dot calls a member of staff over. "Could you do a poached egg for my son? He's been fussy ever since he was little, but what can you do?"

At this point I throw a complete tantrum and spill coffee on my trousers.

Tuesday 30th January: Basque Terror Hits Lemon Curdistan

Wedding anniversary. Up at 5.30am to let the cat in, and stayed up to avoid any danger of an early hippopotamus ambush. Instead, put on bathrobe, logged on to the Internet and looked at the Taipei stock market report. Must have fallen asleep, no mean feat on a typist's chair, because the next thing I knew a crushing weight had descended on my lap. I awoke with Eunice astride me, in a black basque and fishnet stockings, the kind of Kevlar and lace ensemble you would get if Ann Summers had won the contract to build the Millennium Dome.

"We've never actually inaugurated the den have we?" she purred, as the chair creaked ominously.

"Can't…breathe," I gasped, groping beneath the seat for the height release lever. The sudden drop provided a half second of weightless relief before the chair tipped, spilling me backwards onto the carpet of Lemon Curdistan and throwing Eunice against the desk. A cut head, a feminine snivel and the inevitable migraine successfully poisoned the erotic potential for the rest of the day.

Elevenses: While on the carpet had noticed an aged jaffa cake under the desk by the skirting board. Sneaked back later to have it. As hard as a monk's divan and half the flavour.

Later. Muted dinner at the local trattoria. Eunice was delighted with her pearl earrings (should have been for the price), and quite forgave me the earlier tumble. I received a Marks & Spencer tie, and an overly-illustrated book, Sixty nine ways to spice up your marriage by Dr Myron Messiah and Dr Myra Kaplan-Messiah. Got indigestion before I'd finished the dust jacket.

Friday 2nd February: Blair's Tanfield Boost

News of interest: Following a savage and unprovoked mauling of a junior minister (who has since had to be destroyed), hear that John Humphrys has been muzzled under the Dangerous Interviewers Act 2006. Recent police raids have resulted in other seizures, including a Paxman Terrier, famed for its biting sarcasm.

Never mind that Tony Blair is being harassed by the rozzers over the supposed selling of peerages, he found time today to visit my milk float maker Tanfield, who just announced a big order from Marks & Spencer for zero emission vehicles. Tanfield shares added 5p immediately, bringing returns since I bought it in August to 166.6 per cent! Bernard, you old dog, for once you might actually have caught the gravy train at the start of the journey rather than just before it hits the Bisto buffers!

Saturday 3rd February: Ethical M&S

While reading the *FT* over breakfast, Eunice announced she would like to make an investment. Astounded, I looked up to see her waving a Marks & Spencer brochure on ethical funds.

"I picked this up while buying your tie," she said. "I think we'd make more money, fairly and decently and without ruining the planet, than by having you grubbing around arms firms like some latter-day Krupp."

Furious. Absolutely spitting!

Sunday 4th February: Currying Favour On Eunice's Birthday

Eunice is 59 today. After the grief I got last year over the Homer Simpson mug tree, I thought I would shop more effectively online, and I got more ideas in two minutes on the Internet than a whole dreary day on the high street. Memo to self: don't buy retail shares. *The Illustrated Raffia Encyclopaedia* would, I thought, help in the basket-weaving class, while the best-selling bodice-ripper *Seduction in the Seraglio* by Jocasta Lingam would perhaps divert her other appetites. However, after promising two-day delivery, Amazon tangled me up on Friday by correcting to 4-6 weeks for the basket book. What else could I get? After the 2006 nightdress disaster, I wasn't going to rush out to buy clothing, and despite Harry Staines' advice to buy something called a 'Rampant Rabbit', I wasn't going anywhere near Ann Summers. I did think of a cappuccino machine, but the price, the space and of course the fact that I prefer Nescafé rather worked against it. So, when offering Eunice my apologies over breakfast this morning I offered to buy her a new fridge, seeing as ours burps like a scouser and keeps piddling on the floor.

"Why is a fridge a present for me, Bernard? Don't you eat?"

"Of course, but more of your kind of foods go in the fridge. Mine have preservatives, as you never cease to tell me. A Club biscuit can last for months in the Hornby drawer but a bag of spinach turns into a fungus fiesta in a day and a half."

29

Reluctantly, Eunice agreed to have the fridge, so we'll go out to choose one in a week or so.

11pm. Took Eunice to a posh new Tandoori. Pigged out on spicy chicken chat, lamb pasanda, prawn dhansak, an aloo gobi, two glasses of Kingfisher each and a kulfi to finish. My cunning plan, costing £56.80 excluding tip, was to render her too full for nocturnal manoeuvres, hippo or otherwise. It failed: "But Bernard, it's my birthday." Where does she get the energy? And why pick on me? Come on Tanfield, let's get zero-emission vehicles back into the south-east so she can milk a milkman every month or two and give me some peace.

Monday 5th February: Family Plot

Awoke with a vindaloo anvil under my ribs. Got up, let the cat in, wiped up around the fridge while it belched at me, and then into the den to read the BAe Systems annual report. How important this ragbag company, with our shares now worth £614,000, has become to our family's future. Still have no idea how to change Dot's cast iron resolve not to sell, diversify or deal with the inheritance tax calamity that is lurking down the road. I'm beginning to think I have no alternative but to speak to her doctor and get her 'put away'. I feel so guilty even considering it, but it's going to happen one day. Why not before BAe issue a profit warning?

Tuesday 6th February: The Car That Flu Passed

Was driving along the M25 when overtaken by Bernard Matthews in a speeding Jaguar. Well, presume it was him with the personalised number plate H5N1. Have we all been twizzled by the cunning former insurance salesman, though? Seems he's been importing turkey breasts from Hungary, but had always claimed everything was reared in East Anglia. If his company was a PLC then the shares would sag faster than a sneezing turkey, but as a private company, Bernard Matthews can stick two fingers up so long as sales don't collapse. They might yet. Look at how Cadbury got panned from a tiny recall of salmonella-infected chocolate in August. That cost £20m, most of it on advertising, telling people not to eat the chocolate.

One thing you can always rely on is the good old Ministry of Ag to make everything even worse. Since the 2001 foot and mouth epidemic, a new verb, to defracate, has been coined by the OED for the over-enthusiastic precautionary slaughter of farm animals. I'm sure Tony Blair must be itching to reshuffle some ministerial posts and put the health department under Defra. Once the vets in white suits and wellies get to work, he'd never have to worry about waiting lists again.

Elevenses: Nothing whatever in the Hornby drawer. No biscuits in the tin except Ryvita, no sweets anywhere except a solidified packet of Hall's Mentholyptus. Misery.

12.17pm. A postcard from Astrid! She's going to be in London for the weekend of March 30th now she's finished her modelling course. She wants to buy me lunch for helping her escape the traumas of the O'Riordans! Did she know that the Sunday is my birthday? How wonderful!

Close of play: Tanfield climbing again, while BAe at 420p seems to be completely over that bout of nerves about the Al Yamamah fraud inquiry which hit it in December. Some good luck at last!

Chapter Four

Private Iniquity

Wednesday 7th February: Two Wheeler Dealers

Share club meeting. New Canadian member Cynthia Valkenberg dressed down for the Ring o'Bells, in jeans and sweatshirt, but still brought a flashy laptop and chequebook for the first £10,000 of her contribution. While she and K.P. Sharma sorted out the details, Martin Gale and Harry Staines whispered how they'd raised £4,300 by selling the BMW motorcycle they 'liberated' from the container washed up in Devon. While in the gents, they revealed plans for what Harry called a lads' weekend away for the male members of the share club to do some 'research'. This sounds highly unsavoury, so I'm definitely game.

Elevenses: Bought a KitKat on the way to the pub. First chocolate for at least a week. I feel like Robinson Crusoe, macarooned on a dessert-free island. Once back home, vacuumed out the Volvo to remove any crumbs, wrappers or receipts in case of a raid by the Sugar Stasi.

Sunday 11th February: Estate Planning Goes Wrong

Took my mother to the local Isleworth community centre for a special old folks event, with music by 'Doon Ray'. Jemima, who hasn't seen her gran for months, decided to come too. If we can keep Dot happy, perhaps she will let me sell some of those damn shares. Fat chance! While Rupert Murdoch is currently splitting shares in his galactic media empire amongst assorted progeny for tax reasons, my own mother seems determined to commit financial hara-kiri with all of us in tow.

The community centre was just five minutes from Dot's house, so she rode 'Maurice', her mobility vehicle. Every time we stopped to cross the road she'd ram the damn thing into the back of my legs. On arrival, found the place packed. Maurice was left in the corridor and we could only get seats at the back, amongst a tangle of walking frames, wheelchairs and lolling guide dogs.

"Look, Bernard, there's smoked salmon!" Dot rasps into my ear. "And prawns, probably in a marie rose sauce. I hope there'll be some left. We were sent a tin of salmon in 1943 by Aunty Mo in Winnipeg, but the U boats got it. They only let the Spam through because Hitler was allergic to it."

Dot, who can't read her own post or find her teeth in the morning, can spot a canapé at 200 yards, and is already getting agitated about her poor position in the starting grid. Still, there's the music to endure first. The first chords of *Delaney's Donkey* already have Jemima grimacing.

"That's never Val Doonican," Dot says. "They said it was Val Doonican."

"I think he's a Val Doonican tribute act, Mum."

"But I paid £4.50 and it isn't even him!"

"Mum, I paid for the tickets. And if it was Val Doonican I imagine it would be £45 each, not £4.50."

The folksy racket finally runs its whimsical course, leaving only the Schumacher-like revving of pacemakers as 170 pensioners eye the food. One old dear hasn't waited for the signal (the arrival of plates) and is already piling sandwiches into her handbag.

"Where's Gran?" Jemima asks. Dot has disappeared, but only for a moment. She bursts in through the double doors on Maurice, and heads straight for the food tables, scattering the meek and infirm. Blessed they may be, but they'll be lucky to inherit an egg sandwich. Dot is soon at the table, scooping up sausage rolls and vol-au-vents into the handlebar basket, and with the plate of smoked salmon at the far end clearly in her sights. However, it was when the tablecloth got caught in the brake lever that disaster unfurled.

I didn't mind paying the £28.75 bill for the broken crockery, but it was the looks of blame aimed at ME by the community centre staff that I found really hard to bear. And Dot still refuses to sell any BAe shares.

Monday 12th February: Freezing Fiasco

Shopping for a replacement fridge, my birthday treat for Eunice. A disaster, of course. Having already spent an hour in traffic, arrived at Comet superstore just as a gigantic hailstorm began. The car park, about the size of Manitoba and twice as icy, offered not a single vacant space within polar expedition reach of the door. With ice pinging off the car, I suggested bivouacking our support vehicle in the disabled parking area. Eunice refused, instead determined to stage a solo crossing. I dropped her off at the door, and eventually found a slot near the exit between a Hillman Husky and the glass recycling bank. Almost blinded by hail, and with my ears stinging, I reached the door of this winter blunderland with considerable relief.

Eunice, with greasy Comet assistant in orbit, was working her way up an aisle of gigantic fridges, looking at each in turn as if it was an identity parade for some appalling cold-hearted crime. "That's the one," she finally said as I arrived, tapping the door of a silver model the size of a phone box.

While I looked in horror at the price tag, the assistant started to list its features. I took Eunice aside. "Look, dear, we don't need anything this size, do we? There's just the two of us."

"Bernard, you forced me into buying a fridge, so I'm getting the one that I want. I want an ice-maker, and a bigger freezer compartment…"

"Not to mention the rack for a dozen bottles of chardonnay and pinot grigio. You'll never be sober. And this," I said, pointing to the electronic display screen on the door. "Why do we need to know the ambient temperature in Tasmania, or how to tune into Radio Droitwich? It's completely redundant."

"Bernard, you're just being mean. If a fridge is to be a gift it has to be more than functional. And this is."

Tuesday 13th February: Clintonomics

Awoke from a dream about Astrid dressed as a traffic warden who was in the process of pinning a stick of celery to my windscreen. What can this mean? Only six weeks to go and I can ask her!

10am. Hunting through Clintons cards for a suitable Valentine's Day card for Eunice. Requirements: Amusing, affectionate, not containing an ounce of excuse for amorous activity, and above all, cheap. An impossible combination. Actually found one embossed with mating hippopotamuses (£2.79), but don't imagine Eunice would appreciate the joke.

Once a stock market wonder, Clintons is trading at half the peak price of two years ago, but until there are bargains within, I can't consider the shares. Finally settle for a card in the remainder bin at 79p (one corner bent) saying 'things could be worse' which when opened shows a photo of a grinning John Prescott in a leopard skin thong. That should put her right off.

Wednesday 14th February: Contrarian Valentine

Over breakfast, it was clear Eunice was not impressed with the John Prescott card, or the bunch of lilies I bought her as a last minute gesture. "Lilies are for funerals, for the death of innocence, Bernard. Didn't they have any roses left at the filling station?"

Yes they did, but a single one at BP on Curranbridge roundabout cost more than two litres of unleaded. The lilies, by contrast, were on special offer with a free condolence card (which I have hidden away for future use).

I couldn't believe what Eunice had got me. It was a large heart-shaped box of what appeared to be plain chocolates. "Close your eyes, let me feed you one," she said, taking off the lid. This immediately made me suspicious. Eventually, she pinched my nose and I had no choice. It was awful, like an old slipper coated in glue, and would not go down. As I retched, she scolded me: "Bernard, stop this ridiculous fuss and SWALLOW. They're made of quinoa and Korean black bean curd with dried green tea for antioxidants. They're quite delicious."

"Yuurgh," I responded, choking.

"All the ingredients are ethically-sourced."

"Guurgh!"

"Bernard, it's 100% organic!"

"UrggHHH!" I said, trying to slap my own back.

Eunice took over, lecturing me between blows. "Each centre...has a different balance...of essential vitamins...and minerals." Something nasty finally flew out and splattered on Brian and Janet's wedding photograph.

"Bernard, stop retching at once. You have done this quite

deliberately. You won't eat anything from the health food shop, will you?"

Close of play: Peter Edgington phoned to share his latest pearls of wisdom. "Do you know, Bernard, how many TV programmes attacking Tesco there have been in the last week?" he asked. There were apparently five, and he's now convinced that the middle classes have so swung against supermarkets that investors should watch out. "I don't know if anyone in your share club has the shares, but you should let them know," he warned.

Friday 16th February: Minced Profit Pies

Scouring the Internet at 7.15am, stumbled on news that Inter Link Foods, AIM-listed maker of a million mince pies, has issued a profit warning. This is one of Harry's stocks, and knowing his late nights and hard drinking I know he won't be up yet. I ring his house to warn him and wake Avril, Harry's long-suffering wife.

"Hang on. Harry's in the bath," she says.

A moment later I hear a slurred voice on the line. "Wassup?"

"It's Bernard. Are you alright?"

"Fine, fine. Just waking up."

"Avril said you were in the bath."

"Yeah, I must have slept here after getting back from The Harrow…"

"Well, never mind. Inter Link Foods has issued a profit warning and the shares are down 70p at 275p. I thought you'd want to know."

Harry groaned. "After eleven pints of Spitfire last night, three packets of pork scratchings and a lamb bhuna I can't handle a conversation about mince pies." He thanked me and hung up. Something told me he wouldn't get round to selling.

Saturday 17ᵗʰ February: Old Orchard

Drove past the Old Orchard. Bulldozer gone, no sign of house building activity. Fence trodden down. Very strange. Perhaps my complaint to the council has worked?

Sunday 18ᵗʰ February: Old Smartiepants

Brian and Janet came over for lunch with grievous grandson Digby. Eunice, now rejoicing in the role of organic oberleutenant since my high cholesterol results, baked a hideous red cabbage and chard flan topped with figs and sunflower seeds. Even Brian had trouble levering that down his *Guardian*-reading gullet. Digby, of course, wouldn't touch a bite, and when told he couldn't have his Smarties instead, maintained a pout like a slapped supermodel throughout the meal.

Smarties! While Eunice and Janet discussed the latest developments in fallopian tubes over the washing up, and Brian tutted his way through a recent copy of *Chronic Investor*, I stole out into the hall where I found the ill-behaved imp's jacket. In one tiny pocket I found a whole box of Smarties, barely started. Just took one, the first morsel of sweetness for ten days. Then another. After the third and the fourth I was hooked. Guilt was overcome by recalling just how many of *my* chocolate digestives Digby had nicked from the Hornby drawer, I tipped the box into my cardigan pocket. As an afterthought dropped three brown ones (my least favourite) back in the box before returning it.

7.30pm. Waving goodbye to our visitors, watched as Digby donned his coat and opened his box of Smarties. His look of puzzlement was a wonder to behold, until Janet spotted the object of his attention.

"Digby!" said his mother. "You greedy thing! That packet was new this morning. Right, that's it. Give me those. We're rationing you from now on."

Welcome to the regime, Digby. Only three score years and a bit to go.

Monday 19th February: Reversible Door

A gigantic Comet lorry reversed all the way up Endsleigh Gardens to deliver our fridge. With the box it would barely fit through the front door, and once unpacked in the kitchen it dominated the room like a newly materialised Tardis. The only location it would fit made it impossible to open the door fully, but that didn't stop Eunice stacking it with arms full of food from the other fridge.

"This is ridiculous," I said. "You need arms like an orangutan to reach the milk from this side."

"It's alright," Eunice said brightly. "The instructions say the door is fully reversible in three minutes."

"Yes, and no doubt we will then be able to store some winged pig within," I answered with a snort.

Two hours later, I was lying on the kitchen floor with screwdriver in hand. I had already removed the door, skinned my knuckles re-routing the cable to the pointless display from right to left, inverted the top hinge and done various obscure manoeuvrings with almost-but-not-quite identical plastic fittings.

"Now," said Eunice, "Part 17b. It says here...oh no, the rest of this page is instructions in Polish and Croatian. Ah yes, the English instructions continue overleaf. Now it says 'insist the boss B into the recess G who balance the door steady'. Okay?"

"Insist? What do they mean insist? Where was this bloody thing made?" I asked.

"Slovenia, apparently."

"Almost a thousand quid and they can't write a bloody simple instruction in English. We shouldn't let them into the EU until they pass an English test."

"I expect they mean 'insert'."

"Bloody Comet! I've got a bloody good idea where to insert it. Look. I need four arms here. You be the part 'who balances the door steady', and I'll do the bloody 'insisting'." Finally, we managed to balance the door in the correct position.

"Now, part 18," Eunice boomed. "It says 'Insist the reversible alternate flange whom is supplied'."

"What flange? Do you have it?" I asked.

"No. Isn't it amongst those parts?" Eunice said pointing at a selection of plastic widgets by my head.

"No, no. It will have to be metal, won't it? It's a load-bearing part."

"Don't get ratty with me, Bernard. There's nothing metal here," said Eunice, letting go of the door, which fell off, almost crushing me. Worse, it neatly sheared off the boss B which I had just 'insisted'. At that point I just blew my top, and 'insisted' the screwdriver into the door display, which shattered. One broken birthday present.

Chapter Five

Bounced Czech

Tuesday 20th February: Saab Story

Something else for me to cry about. Saab, twenty per cent owned by BAe, is being investigated over bribes by the Czechs. A tip-off from guess who? The Serious Fraud Office, who are so clearly miffed they can't get BAe over the Saudi connection that instead they'll go for broke in other areas. We've got to sell some of those BAe shares while they're still worth something, but my daft mother will not listen.

11.45am. So I did it. I finally rang my mother's doctor and said that I thought Dot could no longer safely look after herself. I described her confusion, the fact she still thinks we live in the Blitz, her attempt to drive her mobility vehicle down the M3 and so on. Dr Singh says he will see her, but explains that there will need to be two medical opinions in order to make an application to have her 'sectioned' against her will, and if granted this can only be initially for a 28-day assessment. Appointment on Friday!

Wednesday 21st February: Stained Profits

BAe results beat expectations. Delight that our luck seems to be holding, but fingers crossed for Friday.

Elevenses: A Cadbury's Creme Egg while on the way to the share club. Didn't notice dropped chocolate fragments which melted on the car seat, and thence onto the seat of my trousers.

Speaking of stains, Harry arrived late to face the same question from everyone: Did you sell Inter Link Foods? The answer, as we all guessed was 'no'. The result was that the 70p drop when I had phoned him about the profit warning on Friday grew to 105p by the close. Then to 115p on Monday, to 155p by Tuesday and earlier today to 195p.

"Why didn't you sell?" asked K.P. Sharma.

"I didn't think they'd fall any more," he said.

"Well, Harry," said Cynthia Valkenberg, "you've only been wrong four times, but I guess you'll be right eventually. Like when it's zero."

Harry scowled at the laughter that greeted the remark. "I'm not selling now. It's too cheap."

"Should we buy some for the club account then?" Martin asked, to which we all shouted 'no!' He's beginning to think we object on principle to all his ideas, but all we ask for is one without a financial suicide note attached.

With 2,000 shares, Harry has lost far more than he gained by selling the BMW motorcycle, but he maintains the losses are only 'on paper'. Chantelle buys him a pint to cheer him up, and we know he must be feeling better because he pinches her bottom and asks for a snog.

Cynthia looks shocked. "Are you for real?" she asks him.

"Hundred per cent prime English beef," he says. "Fancy a nibble?"

Friday 23rd February: Appointment With Destiny

Go to Dot's to take her to the doctor, and she's incensed.

She refuses to get in the car in case I "bundle her off to Broadmoor" and insists on going to the surgery in her mobility vehicle, Maurice.

"Why are we going? I'm not ill," she says.

"I'm a bit concerned about whether you can look after yourself," I say, as she bangs the handlebar into my thigh.

"Mum! Look where you're going!"

Dot then overcompensates and steers Maurice over the toes of an entire bus queue. Entirely oblivious to their cries of pain, Dot continues: "You just want my money, don't you? Well, you can't have it. Geoffrey left it to me. And I'm not going into a home."

By the time we get to see Dr Singh and the approved social worker, Mrs Dunkeley, Dot is in a lather of righteous indignation. Unfortunately for me she's articulate, lucid and accusatory, and remembers the phrase 'power of attorney'. Her charge that I only want the money is made with venom.

"Is it true that you are trying to get her to give you money?" Mrs Dunkeley asks, with a penetrating stare.

"No, it's really only a tax-planning exercise, to protect her investments from inheritance tax for her children's sake, and allow us to spread her money into a variety of assets."

The good doctor steeples his hands. "Look, I don't know anything about investment. But I can tell you that Mrs Jones is in remarkable mental shape for her age, and quite able to look after herself. Indeed, the only health factor that worries me is the stress she has been put under over these shares."

Dot then turned to me. "Right, Bernard. I'm going to take care of my own money. If you ever tell me what to do again, my rolling pin will give you worse head injuries than he's got," she says, pointing at the doctor's turban. "And then I'll leave all the money to the RSPCA."

So that's that. I've lost.

Thursday 1st March: Splicing The ISA

8am. Woke up depressed. Recall that we are going for a big dinner party on Saturday night at Irmgard and Nils' house. What joy. Similar level of enthusiasm as if offered front row seats for a Neil Kinnock speech on constitutional reform. Eunice of course, despite a wardrobe creaking with dresses, claims she has "nothing to wear". I suggest that we take a leaf out of Irmgard's book and look for some hessian leftovers outside the mailbag workshop at Maidstone prison. The response is so fierce I have to lock myself in the bathroom for half an hour.

Noon. Eunice once again flourishes the M&S Ethical Fund leaflet, and says she has decided to transfer all the cash from her mini ISA. Built on a bequest from her late mother, the ISA would have grown to £20,000 by now if she hadn't raided it with a regularity and savagery pioneered by the Mongol hordes. This cash has been splashed out on everything from brocade curtains for our bedroom, to a giant new hat for Jemima's (planned but later abandoned) wedding. So today, the ISA is worth the grand total of £4,571.13, half what it started at in 1998. I point out that once subscribed, she won't be able to treat it like a credit card.

"What do you mean, Bernard? Surely you can sell units."

"Yes, but the costs will probably soak up all your profits. The fund is intended for the long-term, 5-10 years."

"Well yes, so were those St. Michael patent leather shoes, but it didn't stop me taking them back when they gave my bunions gyp." So I shrug my shoulders and watch as she fills out the forms.

Friday 2ⁿᵈ March: Metal Guru

6.45am. I'm still in pyjamas when I received a phone call from our newest share club member, Cynthia Valkenberg. "Bernie, the market's going to tank today."

Cynthia, doing what wealthy Canadians apparently do, has been monitoring the Shanghai market since 5am. Today's ten per cent drop is set to bring a sizeable correction, she says. We should apparently sell the club's Billiton shares and buy back later because metals will be worst hit.

"What makes you so sure," I said, putting my toothbrush down and wiping the paste from my mouth. "The market doesn't open for an hour."

"Trust me on this one. Call me on this number in 45 minutes and I'll patch you in with the others," she said.

Good grief, what is going on?

7.30am. When I ring the number, Cynthia has some kind of conference call arrangement from her home office which allows me to hear her, K.P. Sharma, Mike Delaney, Chantelle and Martin Gale. Though K.P. is the secretary, it soon becomes clear who's boss. She gives us ten reasons why we should sell at the opening then berates us for not having a club spread betting account.

"We're set up for long-term investment, not speculation," Mike reminds her.

"A profit's a profit and a loss is a loss," she says. "With this increased volatility we could make a fortune in the next two weeks, using 6,000 on the FTSE as a target for shorting, and a base from which to go long on rebounds. After that you can all go back to being sleepy long-term investors if you want."

Reluctantly we agree to sell, and while K.P. Sharma sets up the sale we await the opening. Sure enough, the screen turns red immediately. The excitement builds as I hear Cynthia urging K.P. on, "Come on, Come on." There's a little cheer when he confirms the sale for a two per cent loss on the day. Over the next few minutes, a little of Cynthia's background emerges. From being a saleswoman in a small brokerage in Vancouver, she moved to New York for Bear Stearns in 2001, and then was an analyst for a fund manager in London for six years.

"Why did you give it up?" I ask.

"I didn't want to. I got shafted in a promotion, sued the bank for sexual discrimination and walked out with a big settlement. Now I guess I just get itchy feet sometimes," she replies.

Saturday 3rd March: Gathering Tainted Fuel

The party was every bit as dire as I expected. Main course, would you believe, was a parsnip and greengage stir-fry with a block of off-white jelly called 'tofu'. Irmgard's views were equally unpalatable when it came to discussing the tainted petrol crisis.

"I've no sympathy for those people who use Tesco petrol just because it's cheap," she said. "They must know full well it's watered down with additives and preservatives, just like their food. Just think, what is happening to their cars now will in the longer term happen to their bodies too."

So that's what to expect, cancer of the catalytic converter.

Chapter Six

Celandine Sunk

Monday 5th March: Valkenberg Vindicated

8am. Market falls sharply again. BAe not too bad, but Billiton, as Cynthia predicted, is hit hard, eight per cent adrift of Thursday's close and six per cent below the level we sold at. Bloody Spirent, of course, the share which I bought at 82p in 2004 and sold at 37p last June for a massive loss, is standing firm at 58p having lost only 2p during this crisis. Seems I was wrong to buy it, then wrong to sell it. Now, presumably, I am wrong to fret about it.

Eunice calls me out to look at her Clio. "I've just driven back from shopping and it wasn't performing at all well. You don't think it was that tainted fuel do you?"

"Not been filling up at Tesco on the quiet?" I laughed.

"No, Bernard, at Waitrose, where I always do."

Suppressing my mirth, I walk out to the car. The acrid stench of burning hits me immediately, and as I kneel down it is immediately obvious from the heat where it's coming from. "Can you smell this?" I ask her.

"Yes, it's the anchovy and black olive tapenade which leaked on the back seat."

"No, it's the stench of burning brake pad," I said. "You've just driven home with the handbrake on."

Elevenses: A Crunchie and a Curtis Teatime Fancy, consumed from the glove compartment of the Volvo. This devious strategy, executed while waiting my turn at Kwik-Fit, was due to frequent enemy reconnaissance in Lemon Curdistan. However, just as my face was filled with fancy, I looked in the wing mirror and almost choked. Emerging from a Mercedes was the titanic figure of Dr Ross, prostate poker and cholesterol militant. I immediately dived to the floor. Too late, she'd seen me.

"Ah, Mr Jones," she boomed. "Why didn't you keep your appointment with the dietician?"

Mouth full of cake, I attempted to sweep all the wrappers onto the floor. "Ummm. I must have forgotten," I said.

She sternly scanned the crumb-strewn seats, the packets in the foot well and the melted icing around my mouth. "Look. You may fool your poor wife, but you can't fool your body. It's struggling, Mr Jones. You could be dead in five years or you could be fit and active. It's down to you."

Tuesday 6th March: Carry Trade

Markets falling again. Now they say the carry trade is unwinding. I really don't get this. Okay, so the Japanese have been lending money on the cheap, and now it's not so cheap. But even after the rate rise it's still a lot cheaper than my old Bradford & Bingley mortgage was.

Wednesday 7th March: Grievous Bodily Harmsworth

Local rag says that Celandine Homes' planning consent has been revoked 'due to irregularities in the application'. Wonderful, wonderful news! The Old Orchard has been saved, and thanks to my whistle-blowing the pear tree on which I carved Amelia Wrigley's name back in 1961 will not now be cut down. I drive over to the site at Old Dorringsfield just to make sure, and slip in over a broken section of fence. Yes, the tree's still there. Thank the Lord! On return, I find a white van blocking in the Volvo. Two beefy individuals, one with long slicked-back hair and a sharp suit, the other in a hard hat and overalls are deep in argument beside it. They ignore my throat clearing. Finally I walk up and say "Excuse me. Would you mind…"

They look up and suddenly my jaw stops working.

"Well, well. If it isn't that prat Jones," says the suit. "Just the fella we wanted to see."

A long-lost fear grips my heart as I look on the aged but still recognisable countenances of Greg and Barry Harmsworth. Bane of my youth, I'd lost count of the number of Wagon Wheels and Jammie Dodgers I lost to these bullies. I only escaped after the eleven plus when I went off to St Crispin's, and they sank into the educational quagmire of the local secondary modern. Greg, in the overalls, I heard had gone into the Parachute Regiment while Barry distinguished himself with similar bravery evicting old ladies from terraced houses to make way for the great concrete multi-storey car parks of the 1960s. I backed away, but Greg grabbed me and shoved me face first into the side of the van.

"Read that, Jones," he says, pointing at the logo on the driver's door. "What's it say?"

"Celandine Homes, a subsidiary of GBH Ltd," I rasp.

"That's right. Greg and Barry Harmsworth. Destined to be part of Bovis Homes, for four million fat juicy quid. But along comes tree-hugger Bernard bloody Jones to ruin our planning application. We've got no time or cash for an appeal. If Bovis pulls out, I'll find a use for you in the foundations of our next mock Georgian executive home. Understand?"

Monday 12th March: Bernard Interred

7am. Up ready for final results of builder Bovis, having slept badly. A week ago, I'd just have been watching for the pre-tax profits and dividend, seeing as it's one of my best-performing shares. Today, as I scan the company's huge press release, I have bigger worries. There, towards the bottom is the news I most feared. 'After due diligence, Bovis has decided not to proceed with the acquisition of Celandine Homes from GBH Ltd.'

So that's it then. Greg and Barry Harmsworth are going to make good on their threat to drop me into an unmarked plot in their extensive land bank. Perhaps I should forget Dot's will and just put my own in order. I daren't tell Eunice, because she'd insist on going to the police. While I'm sure the Harmsworths are well known to the local rozzers, even they can't do much without witnesses to the threat.

Elevenses: Three half-price custard tarts, well past the sell-by date, from the local baker. I consumed them in the Volvo, parked for quiet reflection by the local cemetery. Thought for the day: I'd rather be interred because of dodgy custard than because of the Harmsworths.

Wednesday 14th March: Swing Charting

Drive to share club, watching over my shoulder for Celandine Homes' vans or similar. At Ring o'Bells, Cynthia Valkenberg, trying to make herself heard above *Sky Sports* in the main bar, shows us her chart techniques. This is absolutely baffling to all except K.P. Sharma, the girly swot, who has on the quiet been using it himself. Support, resistance, moving averages and such mumbo-jumbo may tell us a lot about yesterday, but what about tomorrow?

Cynthia's answer was this: "Imagine, Bernard that there is a tug of war on a beach between invisible teams, buyers and sellers. You see the high, low and close from the flag on the rope, which represents the FTSE, but you need more to know who will win. These measures I'm showing you are ways of measuring the footprints left by the teams, evidence of strength, weakness, momentum and capitulation." She then predicts that the FTSE 100 will not close below 6,000 in the current correction, having "tested it twice" but that we could be due something bigger by late summer. She lets slips that she has already made £3,800 from spread betting since the current weakness began.

Driving home, am sure I'm being followed by a white van.

Sunday 18th March: Smothering Sunday

Long-planned family outing for Dot on Mothering Sunday. I packed Brian, Janet, Jem and Eunice in the Volvo with the Antichrist, plus plastic laser pistol, in the rear-facing seat to terrify following traffic. Lunch booked at expensive restaurant in Richmond, theatre in the afternoon. Arrived at Dot's at 11am to find no-one there. A bit worried, so let myself in. No sign of Dot, but on the kitchen table was a newsletter from OAP Outreach, a local charitable group, with some illegible biro notes on it. On a whim, I rang the number and got through to the local coordinator, a robust woman with a brisk manner.

"Mrs Dorothy Jones?" she boomed. "Oh yes, she's off with the Isleworth branch support group on a Mother's Day trip to Weston super Mare."

"What do you mean?" I exploded. "Her whole family's here to take her out for the day. It's all booked. It's been booked for months. She knows all about it."

"Oh, I'm sorry I think we must be mixed up. Jones IS such a common name isn't it? Our Mrs Jones doesn't have much family. She does have a son somewhere, but he doesn't remember her birthday, never rings and only ever comes to see her to beg for money. We do try to help them out on this special day."

"Oh that's appalling," I said. "Can I just check the address…"

"It's very sad actually," she droned, ignoring the request. "Poor Dot's hardly a bean to her name. Richard, our outreach worker, helped her with the Pension Credit application, and we know she is looked after by the local church around harvest festival. But she's doing ever so well for a 90-year old."

"My mother's 90 too," I interrupted. After I had given her the address, she suddenly went silent. Only then did it dawn on me the extent of the calumnies Dot has spread about me. After all the effort I have made for her! And with £650,000 worth of BAe Systems shares she most certainly doesn't qualify for Pension Credit. Immediate smothering perhaps, but not Pension Credit.

Monday 19th March: Jemima Capers

My daughter Jemima, whose movements are as mysterious as a cat, had dinner with us last night for the first time in six weeks. She's apparently been living with us for a year, leaving at 6am and returning (if at all) at 10pm. The only evidence of her passing is Eunice's increased washing load, the vastly increased usage of hot water, and the sheer impossibility of getting into the main bathroom for hours at a time. Compared to that inconvenience, her consumption of bread, cereal and skimmed milk is quite low. It does grate that despite being a well-off young lawyer, she's never paid us a penny in housekeeping.

"So, then, how's Toby?" I asked, going straight to the nub of the question.

"Why do you ask?" she said.

"Well, I just thought, seeing as we've barely spoken for a few weeks I'd take an interest in your life."

"He's not part of my life."

"What do you mean? I thought you were back together again?"

"Silly Daddy, that was in January. We've broken up twice since then. This time for good. I've been seeing Jonathan since March."

"Who's Jonathan?"

"You've never met him."

Eunice gave me a look which said: don't pursue this.

"Well, what about the flat?" I asked. Jemima had only come to live with us because once Toby had stopped paying his share of the mortgage on their vastly overpriced flat in Fulham, she had been forced to rent it out.

"Well, Toby was supposed to get another tenant. I think he has found someone, but I'm not sure."

"When did the last one leave?"

"Christmas, I think."

"Christmas! Jemima, how is the mortgage being paid then?"

"Toby said he'd put some more money in the joint account. He's done some consultancy." She seemed completely relaxed about the whole thing.

"Jemima, don't you think you should get a grip on this? The mortgage could be in arrears," I said, my voice rising. "For goodness sake, you're twenty-six year's old."

"Bernard, she's twenty-eight. Twenty-nine in July," Eunice chimed in.

"Daddy, it's alright, really."

"The point is," I said, "your mother and I are guarantors on that mortgage. If it gets into arrears, they'll come looking for us. When did you last check the mortgage account?"

"Daddy! I really don't know. Toby's got the paperwork." At which point she got up, looked at her watch and announced she was heading out for the evening.

Eunice put a hand on my arm. "Bernard, I know you're trying to do the right thing, but there's no need to behave like a bull in a china shop."

"What do you mean? I was a model of tact and diplomacy. Especially considering Toby hasn't got regular work, doesn't know which way to turn in bed, and is apparently as lax in his fiscal responsibilities too."

"For goodness sake, you sound like Gordon Brown. If she says it's alright, it probably is," Eunice said. "You can't live her life for her."

"Can't we? We've bloody well paid for enough of it. It's just taxation without representation."

Tuesday 20th March: Day Traders

Cynthia was right about the FTSE. The index is heading off upwards, and in her daily 'heads-up' morning share club e-mail, (a brash innovation I'm not entirely happy about) she says that she has made a further £1,800 on spread betting since Wednesday. The rest of us are still holding out against opening a club spread bet account, but Martin's eyes are not the only ones going misty at the mention of such sums. Under Cynthia's guidance, the club repurchased Billiton last week at £10, having sold it at £11.20 two weeks before. At this rate we'll soon be day traders.

Chapter Seven

Gordon Pulls Rank

Wednesday 21st March: Budget Bludgeon

Share club special Budget meeting in the snug at the Ring o' Bells. Having fought for possession of the big TV against the Manchester United fiends in the bar, settle down with a pint of Old Speckled Hen and a packet of prawn cocktail crisps to see how our investments will fare. As soon as it starts I remember how Browned off I get with Gordon's boasting. Thank God it's his last Budget. Not that anyone's paying much attention. Harry dozes off, Martin Gale and Mike Delaney are playing buzzword bingo (Martin has done particularly well with the phrase 'environmental initiative'), and only K.P. Sharma is making notes. Cynthia is away, and Chantelle is painting her toenails. Orange, since you ask, to match her eyeshadow.

K.P. shushes us. "I missed that!"

"Missed what?" Harry says, waking up.

"About gaming duty," K.P. says, shushing Martin again who is disputing Mike's claim of the word 'enterprise' twice in one sentence. At this point the self-styled 'Man U posse' from the bar appear. Hairy bellies protruding menacingly beneath their Rooney, Ronaldo and Giggs replica shirts, they repossess the TV by tuning to edited highlights of last week's scintillating Oldham Athletic vs Uzbekistan under-21 reserves match. So we're none the wiser about gambling duty until K.P. powers up his new wireless laptop. Oh Lord! Rank's down from 232p to 217p in five minutes!

Turns out that Gordon has upped gambling tax contrary to expectations. This is a kick in the Jowell for Tessa's casino plans, as well as trampling my own share club pick under an £8m bill. But will Rank recover or should we sell? We're still in profit, by 5p a share. Fierce debate ensues, in which I say we should hold, and everyone else says sell because tomorrow will be worse.

"We should have sold Rank in December when it was 270p," says Martin Gale, shaking his head and tutting as if he'd predicted today's problem all along.

"You didn't say anything at the time," K.P observed.

"It's no good blaming us, Martin," Harry noted. "You were the one who could have sold iSoft when it was a quid instead of 35p!"

"And you should have sold Inter Link Foods when it was worth four quid not 80p!" Martin yelled back.

What a bunch of losers we are. In the end we buy another round of Speckled Hen and decide to hold for now.

Friday 23rd March: Clearance Sale

K.P. Sharma rings me to let me know that Rank has hit 190p. I agree I was wrong, and we agree to sell. Feel a little humiliated that my only club share pick has bombed after doing so well. However, I take solace that milk float maker Tanfield has doubled since the start of the year and is now over 100p. Having bought at 30p, I'm £7,000 to the good. That puts me up for the year, and (surprise, surprise) ahead of the FTSE for the first time in God-knows-when.

Sunday 25th March: Do Not Adjust Your Set

Jemima was due to spend the weekend with us, but cried off claiming she's got to finish a brief for a partner over the weekend. There was a garbled message on the answer machine for her from Toby and there are clearly some shenanigans going on. I decide, in the joint financial interest of the Jones family, to drop in on Jemima's flat in Fulham. That will be in the afternoon after I've seen my mother in Isleworth, and will be worthwhile if only to check the post for mortgage foreclosure notices.

First, of course there was Dot to drive me mad. She was watching football on TV when I arrived. "This thing's rubbish Bernard, I'm going to get Radio Rentals to replace it…"

"It's not rented Mum, we bought it for you. From Comet. Do you remember?"

"No I don't. But look, the picture's all wrong."

"Looks alright to me. So when did you start watching football, Mum? It's not your thing, is it?"

"Nonsense. I've been watching for ages. Since half past two. There's all those attractive young men with their strong, hairy legs…"

"Alright, Mum," I said hastily. "So you're a Manchester United fan? You know? The team you're watching. In the red tops."

"Oh I don't know. It's Tim Henman I really used to like."

"He's a tennis player, not a footballer…"

"I know that, what do you take me for?" she looked up at me. "He's got nice legs too. I loved the way he used to shout at the referee: 'You cannot be serious.' That's what he used to say. 'You can NOT be serious.' But they were, you know. Those men in the high chairs. Very serious. Then he'd bung his bat at the ground."

"Mum, that was John McEnroe."

"No he was a racing driver, wasn't he? Killed in the same air crash as Glenn Miller."

I took a deep breath. "So what's wrong with the TV, anyway?"

"The colours are wrong. Look at that man's face! It's blinkin' purple."

"I think you'll find the colour is perfectly tuned, Mum. That's Alex Ferguson."

5pm. Arrived at Jem's flat in Fulham. It's certainly looking a little careworn. The bell is hanging off, and there has never been a knocker, so I let myself in with the spare key. I call out Jem's name, but there is no reply. I realise she's not been recently, when I see the heap of post on the mat. As I head on up the stairs I shuffle through and find, as suspected, several urgent looking letters from the bank. However, an odd rhythmic mewing noise distracts me. Thinking a cat must have got in, I open the door into the lounge and stand for a moment, transfixed. Before me is a fat man, about fifty years old, stark naked and hairy as a neanderthal. He is crouching down with his back to me making energetic love, apparently, to our old Habitat glass coffee table. I blink to shake this bizarre image and then notice two feet (not his) like pink epaulettes above each forested shoulder, jerking backwards with each thrust. A rising breathless howl is emerging from the table, where I now realise by deduction that a woman is bent, squeezed double beneath his fleshly impaling. All this, absorbed in a second, is enough for me to step back. Before I can close the door, the man turns and glances at me in horror. "Jesus Christ!" he gasps, without slowing down. Indeed, if anything he speeds up, in time with the ragged gasps from beneath. I put a finger to my lips as I pull the door to. As I pad down the stairs the woman erupts like an orgasmic Vesuvius, and I swear the doors rattle.

I flee to the car, vowing that I will never let Jem know what her aged tenants get up to. My God! How I admired the verve and energy, the sheer desire in that frenzied coupling.

On the way out I notice Jem's car in a side street. How odd. She must be in the vicinity. She'll get a real shock if she walks in on Mr and Mrs Testosterone up there.

Monday 26th March: Serf In The Net

Right across the British Empire, 200 years ago yesterday, slavery was abolished. Except at number seventeen Endsleigh Gardens where the relationship between owner (Eunice) and chattel (me) hasn't changed since the fall of Carthage. Today started at 6am with letting the cat in, drying its muddy paws, attempting to feed the fussy thing, emptying the dishwasher and bringing up a cup of tea to the mistress of the house for eight o'clock.

"Bernard," she says, peering out of the window. "You still haven't mended that pane in the shed window."

"Yes, I was too busy fixing your handbrake..." I started, recalling her attempt to drive home from Waitrose with it half on.

"Look. I've made a list to help you," she said brightly.

This so-called list is more like a regional regeneration project. I'm expected to put up a new outside light, repave the broken patio flagstones, mend the fence which blew down in the gales, re-grout the mouldy tiles in the en-suite bathroom (again) and unblock the outside drain for the second time since Christmas.

"Look I wouldn't have to keep clearing this bloody drain if Jem would just remember to fish her hair out of the plughole when she showers," I said.

"Don't be harsh," Eunice retorted. "Jemima's in a delicate emotional state at the moment since she found Toby had been out to that gay bar.

Elevenses: During a brief pause for breath in this Burma Railway of a household, I consume a whole tube of Smarties, swallowing them rapidly overdose-style with a glass of water for fear of being caught by the guards. Counting off the days (five!) until my lunch date with Astrid. I'll take her to a romantic little Soho place I know. But what excuse can I give Eunice for going up to London on a Saturday, alone?

Chapter Eight

Cosmetic Surgery

Monday 26th March: Tanfield Results

5pm. Completely overlooked Tanfield results this morning in my excitement about meeting Astrid at the weekend. The milk float maker has certainly caught the zero-emission wave, with retailers like M&S and delivery firms queuing up to take its vehicles. However, despite doubled turnover and a bulging order book, I feel the shares are looking a little pricey now at 105p, that's a historic P/E ratio of over 100 and 16 times the forecasted results. Having seen how I slipped up with Rank, I'm tempted to bag my profits as soon as the market opens tomorrow.

Noticed a white van parked opposite the house today. Greasy-haired man inside hiding behind *The Sun* looked suspiciously like Barry Harmsworth of GBH Ltd and Celandine Homes.

Tuesday 27th March: Cosmetic Sector Plunges

7am. There I was minding my own business having a shower, when the suction cups holding up the shelves finally gave way under the Waitrose camomile and jojoba everyday shampoo, Herbal Essences Body Envy Volumizing Shampoo, Mop Basil Full Curl Conditioner, Evelyn & Crabapple exfoliating bloody body scrub with tea tree oil, two tubes of Clearasil, three disposable Ladyshave armpit and shin deforesters and a pumice stone rougher than a barmaid's tongue. Buried alive, and in agony. Eunice responded to my yells for help with all the urgency of NTL customer support.

"Bernard, what on earth are you doing?" she finally said as I inspected my bleeding foot, amid smashed shelving and curdling pools of yellow and green hair goop.

"Bathing in asses milk, what do you think? Would you give me a hand? I think that metal canister of Hairomatherapy conditioner has broken my foot, and I've slashed an artery on the Ladyshave."

As I sat down on the edge of the bath, I pointed out that you cannot expect to cram into one small shower every hair and body care product known to woman. "What on earth do you do with all this? Jojoba and nettle skin rejuvenation? Look at this one: L'Oreal Skin Reincarnation. Are you planning to come back as Queen bloody Nefertiti? You'll need a bloody pyramid if you want all this lot buried with you!"

Spent the next two hours waiting in A&E with a blood-soaked towel round my foot, with Eunice in control of my hospital wheelchair. Finally get to see a quack, who spends all of five seconds telling me what I already know: yes, that is a nasty cut. Can you move this? Yes, it does look broken to me. Then back into the corridor for another two hour wait for stitches and a cast. Back home, still fuming, I decide to research this cosmetics business. It takes one minute on the Internet to see that behind the hype it's pretty basic bulk chemicals: water, a detergent (typically ammonium lauryl sulfate) and a foaming agent usually made of coconut fat, to make lather. No wonder beauty firms like L'Oreal, Revlon and Wella trade on a higher P/E ratio than pharmaceutical companies. They don't spend $800m developing each product and proving their claims to regulators, yet every woman has to have bucket loads of this stuff which costs pounds to buy and pennies to make. Perhaps I should invest, but for a pure play I need to go abroad.

Wednesday 28th March: Excitement Mounts

Share club meeting. While buying a round at the bar, made the mistake of confessing my excitement about this weekend's date with Astrid to that model of propriety and discretion, Harry Staines. As soon as I'd let the word's leave my lips I realised my grievous mistake.

"Hey, lads," Harry called to Martin Gale and Mike Delaney,

who were playing a game of pool that had so far lasted an hour and 40 minutes without a ball being sunk. "Bernie reckons he's going to roger this young au pair at the weekend."

"I didn't say that!" I said to Harry. "What I said was that we are having a romantic lunch together."

"Yeah, yeah." Harry said. "You're not there to discuss Arsenal's latest signing or the drawbacks of precipice bonds, are you? It's all an ABC of technique. Romantic lunch, three glasses of Liebfraumilch, and a bunch of flowers and you're home and wet."

"Sometimes, Harry, you can be too base. Astrid is a really nice girl," I said.

"So was Julia Hinton-Clarke," Harry responded, going a little misty-eyed. "But after three Babychams and a pork cutlet at the Schooner Inn she let me prise her bra off in the back of my Hillman Minx. Further progress was looking a bit iffy, so I rubbed me eyes with a pre-prepared hanky with a bit of onion in it, told her I loved her, and we rounded off the afternoon with a ferocious knee-trembler in the tradesmen's entrance of the Leeds Permanent Building Society. I was back home without missing the football results."

As Mike and Martin abandoned the game of pool (and hid the ripped baize with a beer mat), everyone wanted to see the photo I'd brought. It was taken the summer before with a telephoto lens from our bedroom window and over the recently (and cunningly) trimmed *Leylandii* hedge. It showed a bronzed Astrid in a blue bikini and sunglasses lying asleep on a sun lounger.

"Bloody hell, Bernard, she's fantastic!" Martin gasped. "You lucky sod."

"Quite nice tits," conceded Mike Delaney, brushing cigarette ash off his threadbare and dandruff-decked jacket. "Bit of a shame about the small mole on the left one. And she could probably lose a pound or two, ideally."

"Tragic isn't it," Harry said, pointing to her sunglasses. "...to realise that such a beautiful woman is seriously disabled. Blind, and with no sense of taste." He maintained the straight face until I dug him in the ribs.

"So you're really going to give her one, are you Bernard," Martin said. "No bullshit?"

"Look," I said, exasperated beyond measure. "Astrid and I are good friends, that's all. I helped rescue her from au pair hell with the bloody O'Riordans next door, and bathed her foot which she cut when escaping. I also protected her when Ken O'Riordan tried to smash down our door to get her back."

"Ah well," they concurred, nodding to each other as if it was a sound investment I had made. Harry spoke for them all when he said: "When all's said and done, Bernard, that's a blow job's worth in anyone's money."

Friday 30th March: Excuses, Excuses

"But Bernard, you can't possibly hobble around a model railway exhibition on crutches, you'll be exhausted." Eunice is gradually picking holes in my excuse for going up to London tomorrow for my lunchtime tryst with Astrid. "Look, let me drive you at least. You can't drive and you can't possibly manage the train."

"It's alright, Mike Delaney's offered to drive me," I lied.

"I thought he hated model railways. And think of his smoking in the car..."

Eventually, however, Eunice accepts my plans.

Close of play: Sold my Tanfield shares for 103p!

Saturday 31st March: Two's Company...

Got the train to meet Astrid. Hobbled into the restaurant, heart pounding, and see her there at the bar being chatted up by some revolting youth with unkempt hair. She, however, is as gorgeous as ever and very concerned about the foot. Even after I hug her, the fellow doesn't take the hint, and just grins at me. "Hi, I'm Lars," he says.

"Very nice, I'm sure. You will excuse us while we move to the table," I say to him. "We've not seen each other for months. But perhaps you would be good enough to get me the wine list?"

"Oh no, Bernard!" Astrid smiles. "I'm so sorry I didn't introduce you. Lars is my fiancé. Did I not mention this in the e-mail?"

At the end of a very uncomfortable three-way meal, Astrid takes me aside and says. "Perhaps this wasn't a very good idea. We couldn't ever be what I think you want us to be. Oh Bernard, you are a very sweet man, but whatever were you thinking?" Then she kisses me on the forehead, and sweeps out of my life forever.

Sunday 1st April: Birthday Blues

My 64th birthday. Despite my advancing years and plaster cast, Eunice awoke me at 7.30am to inflict a hippopotamus manoeuvre. Got told off for "not making an effort", but it was about as erotic as being trapped under a storm-lashed bouncy castle. I was certainly making an effort to breathe.

Other gratuities were more random. A giant green cardigan from my mother (which was doubtless intended to double as a tent in case a doodlebug got the house), a Thomas the Tank Engine tie from sister Yvonne, and a Hornby coal truck from my increasingly clever grandson Digby. Opened the box to find he had filled the wagon with a cellophane packet of Smarties. Perhaps Digby suspects who it was that helped themselves to his Smarties? Or perhaps he just feels sorry for me. I know I feel very sorry for myself after yesterday's fiasco with Astrid. I'm an old fool, entertaining the idea she might have feelings for me beyond pity.

Family lunch did little to raise my spirits, though Eunice baked me a giant jam sponge with lashings of custard as a special exception to the cholesterol rule.

"I hope you enjoy it, Bernard. But given your condition I've been a bit careful. It's diabetic jam and skimmed milk."

What condition? I don't have diabetes. Is she referring to my terminal bloody misery? Do they do a jam for that?

5pm. Peter Edgington phoned. Perfect Peter, whose portfolio regularly beats the FTSE by five points a year, spent more time congratulating me on my stock picking than on my advanced age.

"Well done on Tanfield. Just 30p, is that all you paid? And now 110p. I'd have been proud indeed to have made that pick."

However, when I told him I'd taken profits at 103p, he was aghast. "Why, Bernard? It's got plenty more juice left in it. You've got to run those profits, not just to the point when it's fully valued but when the crazy people start buying. Wait until you see it written up in the *Express* or the *Daily Star*. That's the moment to let go."

That's all very well for him to say, but I held on to Rank too long for the share club, and all my profits ebbed away. I'm not taking chances any more.

Chapter Nine

Courting Trouble

Tuesday 3rd April: Court Appearance

Feeling very sorry for myself. The long-delayed and long-deferred court case of driving without due care and attention from last year finally hit the magistrates court, though hit is rather an exaggeration for something slower than continental drift. Had to be there at 10am, but not 'processed' until 3.30pm, by which time Eunice had long given up to go shopping and even Jemima said she had to go back to work. All that time I was unable to escape the droning protestations of one Kealey, a wretched careworn single mother awaiting prosecution for affray. To listen to Kealey talk about her family, and for five whole hours I had little choice, was to hear about four sons and two daughters who were the very cherubim and seraphim of holiness. Their sixty-two collective convictions for breaking and entering, handling stolen goods, actual and grievous bodily harm, soliciting, possession of class A and B drugs and their own personalised ASBOs were all, according to Kealey, due to error, mistake, bureaucratic persecution and the malice of neighbours. By the time my case was called I'd have pleaded guilty to mass murder just to escape sitting next to her.

Things did not improve however, once I was in the courtroom. The prosecuting solicitor turned out to be Nigel Uttley-Fullership, who I recall being the ultimate smug prefect at school. My own solicitor, having promised to turn up in person, cried off sick with, of all things, conjunctivitis. In his place he dispatched (possibly by post) one Ms Sarah Semple, a pale and inert stick insect who looked not a day over seventeen, and made Kate Moss seem obese. Barely able to lift her document cases, Ms Semple made eye contact only with her papers, and her voice could not be heard over the extractor fan, which at times threatened to suck her from the courtroom.

Ms Semple was like a moth fluttering in the path of Uttley-Fullership's steamroller of sarcasm. I however, took its full weight.

Yes, I'd lost a wing mirror on the rented removal van. Yes, I couldn't see the other mirror because a large stuffed pig called Prescott was in the way. Yes, the pig was restrained by the seat belt, rather than my daughter. Yes, I'd heard the police helicopter, and the sirens. Yes, I'd taken an illegal left turn off a dual carriageway by driving in the hard shoulder and then over the verge. Yes, I'd probably exceeded the speed limit. Yes, I'd not stopped when lights were flashed at me by a following police motorcycle. Finally, he asked me. "Mr Jones, I'm having trouble with some of the fuzzy documents here. Would you be able to remind the court of your date of birth."

"First of the fourth," I responded, using the shorthand I always employed.

"April 1st, Mr Jones. Would you please remind the court of the popular nomenclature attached to that date."

"All Fools day, if that's what you're driving at."

"No further questions."

"I have one," I said, turning to the stipendiary. "Is it possible to change my plea to guilty?"

Wednesday 4th April: An Arresting Experience

Overslept until 8.45am. Woke up to the revelation that my three penalty points and £200 fine were not a dream, but a piece of wretched reality. Grumbling my way to the bathroom I discovered I had run out of toothpaste. Calls for Eunice's assistance were not answered. No sign of Jemima either. Burrowing through cupboards, found some of Jemima's Body Shop toothpaste, which looked okay but seemed to be celery flavour with a stripe of beetroot, and left a disgusting tang in my mouth. No hot water left for a shower (how can I tell that Jem stayed overnight?) so settled for a tepid scrub at the basin. On return to the bedroom found that Eunice had organised a major clearance in the 'smalls' department. Most of the contents of my underwear drawer were now dumped in the linen basket for washing, and the only thing left to wear were those disgusting Marks & Spencer tartan boxer shorts which she bought me one Christmas. Digging through the socks for some alternative, the only thing I found was that ridiculous wet-look posing pouch Eunice bought me for my birthday in 2004, and had forced me to wear. Finally decided that the memories of that allegedly romantic evening were too unpleasant to be faced, and struggled into a pair of the giant kilt-like M&S creations. Downstairs was a note in which Eunice said she and Jem had gone shopping and would rendezvous with me later.

12.45pm. Arrived at the Ring o'Bells for share club meeting. Main bar seemed packed, but the place went oddly quiet as I arrived. Remarked on this to Harry Staines, who admitted he'd told all and sundry my story about the tangle with the Met, and the subsequent prosecution. A number of people seemed in the know that it had recently been my birthday, so had a row of drinks lined up. It was almost 1pm but no-one seemed to be in a hurry to go into the back bar, indeed Harry detained me with one last joke. Suddenly the pub door opened behind me, and you could hear a pin drop. I turned around and two young and extremely pretty policewomen were heading straight for me.

"Bernard Jones, we've got a warrant for your arrest."

"Oh for God's sake, not again," I cried.

"You are not obliged to say anything..." At which point the blonde one whipped out a pair of handcuffs and pinned my wrists behind me. The other took off her cap, and flicked out a cascade of wavy dark hair, at which point music began and a great cheer went up from the bar. She then started to kiss me! The blonde pulled my jacket down to my arms, then my shirt. They both began an incredibly seductive strip, down to camisole, stockings and g-strings, whooped on by the others. Once I overcame my shock I started to enjoy myself, until the dark one said: "Well, Mr Jones, we have to take down your particulars." She dropped to her knees and undid my belt.

"No, don't," I pleaded, but the trousers came off. I tried to turn to the bar, but it was no good. The loose tartan boxers did nothing to hide my excitement.

"Hoots, mon," Harry shouted. "Toss his caber, girls!"

At this point, with the blonde's hands drawing down my waistband, I really started to plead. I noticed Harry handing a wodge of cash to the dark one, whispering instructions in her ear.

"Don't you dare," I shouted, adding a few expletives for good measure. Martin Gale then hove into view with a camcorder on which my embarrassment was recorded, from every angle as the cheers roared in my ears. Finally I slipped to the filthy nut husk and crisp-strewn floor, without my boxers and with two semi-naked young women grappling to retain a hold on any part of me that came to hand. It was at this point that I heard the door open and an absolute silence descend. The one word, familiarly expressed, was all I needed to know that my life would now not be worth living: "BERNARD!"

Thursday 5th April: Solitary Confinement

Perhaps I should do this more often. I am in solitary confinement, moved to the spare room, something I have tried to achieve for years. Eunice has not spoken to me for thirty-six hours, another plus. The downsides are that I have to prepare my own meals, do my own washing, make the bed and clear up after myself. This is not, in fact, too high a price to pay for a wordless huff that

I'm hoping Eunice will extend for several weeks yet. It doesn't seem to have dawned on her that I was not in any way responsible for any of the events that happened at the Ring o'Bells yesterday. As I had attempted to explain to a sceptical and outraged Eunice, these two beautiful strippers were forced upon me by circumstances I was powerless to control. It was, I must admit, the most delicious entrapment.

Close of play: Jem came up into the loft to express her sympathies for my predicament, but looking round at the two locomotives chugging around the track, the half-eaten box of Maltesers and the portable TV soon realised why I wasn't at all glum.

"It really looks like you're enjoying yourself, Daddy," she said, chuckling to herself. "You've got everything you need here. I don't think Mummy realises that this isn't punishing you at all."

"I'd be grateful if you didn't let her know that fact, Jem," I said. "She'll only think of some other more effective form of torture. Like trying to talk through our relationship, force me to confront my inner angst or some other psychobabble nonsense."

"Mummy is dedicated to your marriage. She'll never give up trying to get you to treat it as something worthwhile, rather than something to be skirted around."

Chapter Ten

Knuckle Sandwich

Friday 6th April: Good Friday For Some

Up in town to meet some of the old MoD crowd for a meal at Simpson on the Strand. Arrange to meet Jem for a drink beforehand in a pub near her office. She is late as usual, and looks a little harried.

"Great to see you," I say, getting up from my bar stool for a hug, only to receive an indifferent 'air kiss'.

"How are you?" I ask, after I've bought her the requested double G&T.

"Fine."

"Work going okay?"

"Fine."

"How's the love life?"

My daughter looked sideways at me and flicked her hair. "Well probably not as exciting as yours has been in recent days."

"And Jonathan, are you still…"

"Good grief, Daddy. Has Mummy sent you on a spying mission? All these questions! And not very subtle ones, either."

"Alright," I respond. "How about a Daddy-type question? Did Toby get some tenants in for the flat so that you can meet the mortgage payments?"

"No, he's been an absolute twit. He keeps forgetting to organise it. At least he had the good grace to make a couple of mortgage payments though."

At this I did a double take. "So there's been no-one in at all?"

"That's what I just said."

"And you've not let an estate agent or anyone have the key?"

"Daddy, what are you on about? There are only three keys. Toby's got one, I've got one and yours is the third. Why? What's the matter?"

"Ah." The vision of the hairy-backed thruster intruded into my mind. Jem kept looking at me for explanation, but something held me back. Just at that moment I heard someone approach, and watched Jem's eyes flick up over my shoulder in recognition.

"Jonathan," she said "This is my father. Daddy, this is Jonathan. He's the senior partner I work under."

As I turned to greet Jonathan, the truth of this last assertion suddenly rang true. His hairy, pudgy hand pumped mine briefly until the recognition dawned on us both, and his easy smile melted away. The conversation dawdled slowly until Jem went off to the loo, and Jonathan spread his hands expressively.

"Mr Jones, I'm most terribly sorry…"

"I suspect not, actually. Except for being caught. You didn't say anything to her, did you?" I said. "She still doesn't know I saw you both."

He shook his head, slowly.

"Best not to, then. Under the circumstances," I added.

He nodded, and looked down at his hands in the nearest to contrition I'd ever seen on a lawyer. As I too looked down at his hands, I noticed a wedding ring.

"You bastard," I said. I was quite surprised to notice my right fist, seemingly of its own accord, launch itself across the table and crunch into his nose. My God, I've just punched someone! For the first time in decades. Not just anyone, but a senior solicitor who probably charges £500 an hour. And I enjoyed it. Jonathan lurched, and as blood began to run, patted his pockets desperately for a handkerchief. I offered him mine.

"I'm so sorry," he honked.

"We'll consider the matter settled then, shall we?"

"Nnghh," he assented, through an increasingly crimson cloth.

"There's no need for your wife to know about this, is there?"

"Nnghh," he shook his head slowly.

"And my daughter's career prospects will remain pristine?"

"Yefff…"

"As well as her honour, from now on?"

He nodded.

"Then I leave you to make whatever explanations are required when she returns from the ladies. Perhaps you can tell her I had to leave for another engagement. Sorry about your nose, by the way." Then I walked out, feeling utterly triumphant.

Thursday 12th April: Hell Your Mamma

BAe Systems is eating away at my brain. At 465p, the shares my mother holds are still worth over £600,000, representing the biggest inheritable asset in the Jones family. Yet I have this horrible feeling the OECD and now the U.S. are so incensed at Britain dropping the fraud inquiry into BAe's Saudi arms deal that some legal measure is likely. One only has to think of the online gambling sector to see how the U.S. can punish companies. If only Dot would let me sell some shares to diversify this liability. But no, she's adamant that somehow I'm trying to diddle her. Having failed to get her 'sectioned', or get power of attorney, I've got to the stage now that I would hack into her broker account to rearrange her portfolio if it were possible. I know she never uses the web-based version, she has enough trouble dialling the telephone broker, and I know the account number, but not the password. So at 5.30am this morning, after letting the cat in, I padded down to the den and spent 45 minutes trying to type in likely passwords. Got frozen out of the site after six wrong attempts. Must think laterally on this.

Friday 13th April: The Girl From Impetigo

Loitering without intent outside Bhs while Eunice restocked her lingerie hangar, I noticed a new independent bookshop where the old Wimpy Bar had been. This welcoming little place had its own wing chairs, and tea and coffee from a good old-fashioned urn for 90p. None of this gurgling cappuccino Starbucks nonsense. A sixtyish woman behind the desk, all worsted skirt and wing-spectacles, glanced at me and there was some flicker of recognition. As she came up to me, I reluctantly lowered my copy of *Wensleydale Railway: Rolling stock pre-1913*.

"You're Bernard Jones aren't you? I'm Ingrid Pratt. Do you remember? Amelia Wrigley's friend."

Yes, I did remember. I first recalled Ingrid from infants school where she gave me, four-eyes Filton and Bob Snetton playground kisses and, it later transpired, impetigo. She was all of six, but still a "common little hussy" according to my mother. In her teens she used to hang around with Amelia, my first (and greatest) love.

"Did you ever go out to Oz to see Amelia after she emigrated?" I asked.

"No need to. She was back within two years. Last I'd heard she married a Germolene salesman and moved to Orpington."

Good grief! She's been so close, all this time.

Chapter Eleven

Hacking Jacket

Monday 16th April: Stock Screening The Ring o'Bells Way

Inevitably, Tanfield continues to climb despite the sale of a stake by a major shareholder (me). At 122p it's 20p above my sale price, and £2,000 profit foregone. Perfect Peter was, as usual, correct. Still, I have £7,200 in real profits. Now to spend it. I scanned *Chronic Investor* for some appealing opportunities and saw an interesting article on stock screeners. Hadn't heard of them before. Perhaps we should build one for the share club, with the following criteria for any share: Martin Gale must think it's a screaming bargain; Harry Staines must have lost money on it; K.P. Sharma wouldn't touch it with a barge pole; and Cynthia says its chart looks terrible. Then we short-sell it for all it's worth.

Elevenses: Two strawberry and cream-filled meringues on special offer at the local bakery. Eaten, messily, in the car parked outside Argos. Got back home to an interrogation.

"Bernard. You've got cream on your cheek."

"No, that's shaving cream."

"Don't be ridiculous. You didn't have it at breakfast time, I would have noticed. And look, there's a cream stain on your jacket too. Or were you shaving fully clothed, in the car?"

Oh God. Why do I always get caught?

Tuesday 17th April: Cybersprog

Incandescent with fury! Son Brian and grandson Digby came round in the afternoon to collect the spare lawnmower. While Brian and I cracked our vertebrae carrying the damn thing to his car, Digby disappeared. After they had gone, I returned to my PC to check the closing prices. Instead of the desktop's usual icons, I saw a giant picture of the mischievous imp sticking out his tongue, which he had somehow set as the background. He'd also mucked about with fonts, colours and Lord knows what else. It took me two hours to fix it, using a magnifying glass to read the 3pt, canary-coloured Gothic font on lime background. When I rebooted, all my changes were undone! Giving up, I realised I could use our family micro-hacker to break in to my mother's stockbroker account.

Finally checked my share prices on Teletext, after fighting for the remote with Eunice. She was watching *Bay Weightwatch*, some Channel Five nonsense where a dozen obese and mouthy teenagers are put out to sea in a leaking boat and viewers have to text in who they first want lobbed over the side.

Thursday 19th April: Trends And Friends

Called in a man to re-set the PC. It now has a password to keep cyberbrats at bay! Am continuing to outperform the FTSE 100, by two points. While happy with that, am so concerned about 'reversion to the mean', which affects successful fund managers, that am tempted to sell everything to freeze my outperformance. This would be silly, as K.P. Sharma reminded me yesterday, because "The trend is your friend". Well, let's face facts. The trend hasn't been on speaking terms with me for most of the last five years, so I'm hardly likely to trust the bugger now.

Got back to Dot's broker website, in my quest to hack into her account and sell those damn BAe shares. Got nowhere with passwords, so instead I clicked to have a password reminder sent. It came up, astonishingly, with an e-mail option. I verified that, yes, I wanted the password e-mailed not posted. So Dot, somewhere, must have an e-mail address. That gave me an idea. I rang Dot.

"Eeh male?" she said. "What are you on about?"

"It's to do with the Internet. You can send letters to people without having to post them."

"If you don't post them they won't get there," Dot insisted.

"Alright, look. Do you have Clive's phone number?"

Dot sounded baffled, even after I reminded her that Clive was Mrs Harrison's health visitor who helped her set up the account. Only when I mentioned the words 'black' and 'Rastafarian' did she remember who he was.

"Ooh yes. The one you thought was a burglar, and attacked outside the house. When I hit you with a rolling pin."

All in all it took me an hour to get hold of Clive. When I did, I explained that I needed to get the e-mail account active for Dot. Though he recalled setting it up, he couldn't remember any details, but promised to look to see if he had any test messages on his laptop and would phone me back. Promising!

5pm. Peter Edgington called. He is spending some of his ill-gotten gains on a gigantic summer holiday.

"I'm taking the family on the trans-Siberian railway all the way to Vladivostok", he said. "You'd love it Bernard, it's the world's most epic train journey."

Epic? Clearly the man has never tried to get from Tonbridge to Isleworth on a Sunday when there's engineering works.

Wednesday 25ᵗʰ April: Cynthia-sized Share Club

Having missed the last two share club meetings, I reappear to find much has changed. Cynthia Valkenberg, resplendent in magenta jacket, frilly blouse and patent leather shoes, is now firmly in charge. Having poured in her own funds, her wealth accounts for £9 of every £10 in the club. Canada's answer to George Soros has put ten grand each in BSkyB, BT and equipment hire group Ashtead, and smaller stakes in a wide variety of AIM-listed shares including Debt Free Direct and Oakdene Homes. The only one of our own share picks still in the portfolio is Billiton.

"What we really need now is a spread betting account for the club, so we can go short," Cynthia says breezily. There's so much overpriced stuff out there, and May's seasonal weakness should be exploited. We could build a little long-short hedge fund."

While K.P. Sharma and Chantelle are going along with her plans, Mike Delaney is made to stand outside while he smokes, and Harry and Martin Gale have retreated to the other bar to watch Sky's gripping coverage of Malta vs Lesotho women's coxless fours. Harry is disappointed to find that it is rowing not mud wrestling.

"We made a big mistake," Martin says, supping a foaming pint of Throstler's Intestinal Vengeance. "We agreed to let her vote on trading decisions in proportion to her investment. She blinds us with science about charts and then, with this instant majority, tells us what we're going to buy or sell. It's no fun anymore."

"Look at this," says Harry, brandishing a hefty hardback, now coated in pork scratching crumbs. "She wants me to read this for next week: 'The complete guide to point and figure charting'. What a load of old cobblers!"

I try to have a quiet word with Cynthia, letting her know that there is a bit of upset. After all, it's only a hobby and a chance to get away from the house. It should be fun, I say.

"I don't get you guys," Cynthia says. "You expect to make dough without effort. Couldn't you use a couple of thousand pounds, Bernard?"

"Of course, but…"

"Well then, listen to what's on offer. What I've shown you about charting would cost thousands if you took a trading course in the City. I give you guys first class advice and support, and all you do is throw it back in my face. When Eunice asked me to help…"

"Eunice asked you!" I squeaked. "So you're just a spy!"

"Don't be paranoid. I had the money to invest, and when I talked with Eunice at Helena's funeral she said you guys needed a woman's expertise to avoid losing your shirts."

"What!"

"Eunice said to me 'You have to be firm with Bernard. He's easily led and needs strict discipline.' Sure, it's a favour. But if you old British buffers want to play financial shove ha'penny, and nod off in your own drool then I'll take my profits and go elsewhere."

I'm gobsmacked, absolutely gobsmacked.

Saturday 28th April: Debriefing At HQ

Stand up row with Eunice about share club spies, the fourth such ding-dong since the maple leaf Mata Hari was uncovered.

"Bernard, how much money have you personally made in two years since you joined the share club?"

"A few hundred, I expect," I lied (I'm actually down a tad.)

"Lord above, you don't even know! Anyhow, assume £300. Deduct two year's beer, the giant packets of crisps, yes, Cynthia told me, deduct the petrol and what have you left? Nothing!"

Chastened, I took solace in the model railway.

Wednesday 2nd May: John Browne's Body Lies...

The Ring o'Bells, this week minus a sulking Cynthia, is abuzz with news of the resignation of Lord Browne from BP.

"I'm so shocked," said K.P. Sharma. "The most admired businessman of our generation lied under oath! Is there no-one we can look to for moral business leadership?" he said stuffing a handful of prawn cocktail crisps into his mouth.

"Well, there's always Conrad Black," Harry Staines chuckled.

"What interests me about Lord Browne," said Martin Gale, trying to break his record for flipping 28 beer mats from the edge of the table, "is not that he is gay. It is that he lived with Mummy, until she died in 2003. Did she straighten his tie before sending him off to BP every day? Did she make him a packed lunch and put Savlon on his knees? Did she comfort him when the boardroom bullies demanded his tuck? Did she help him with maths homework, calculating his share options?"

I'm as surprised as the others. But what interests me is that Perfect Peter Edgington predicted this. In my diary, in August 2006, I see Peter had made the case for contrarian management cycles, selling his BP shares at 670p when everybody thought Lord Browne could do no wrong. Now they're a pound lower.

Chapter Twelve

Carrot And Stick

Saturday 5th May: The Early Bird

8.30am. Harry Staines rings me in an excited state. For the Ring o'Bells own septuagenarian barfly, this normally means he has managed to machete his way into the cavernous underwear of some superannuated barmaid. However, this is much too early in the day for such boasts. He'd still be getting his breath back. Instead, the share club's very own buy-and-ignore investor has seen a snippet in the *Telegraph*. One of his pack of dog stocks, Inter Link Foods, is in bid discussions with McCambridge Group.

"Take a decko into cyberspace for me, would you?" Harry asks. "I've never heard of McCambridge. It sounds like one of those fast food universities."

A few quick Googles later, and I'm able to tell him it's an Irish firm, the fastest growing baking group in the British Isles, but sales are only £30m, just a quarter of the size of Inter Link.

"Oh," he said, deflated. "They won't be able to afford it then, will they? Inter Link's got £60m of debt."

Who knows? A generation ago, Harry would have been right, but leveraged financing, private equity and the carry trade seem to make anything possible. Someone seems to think it's possible seeing as Friday's share price, 134p, is double the March low of 66p. Still, it's miles below the 350p Harry paid.

Sunday 6th May: A Sunday Roasting

Eunice is preparing Sunday lunch for her vegan friend Irmgard and her inscrutable partner Nils. Not content with making me eat the organic rubbish, I have to help prepare it. So I do my duty, cleaning and paring some very mangy carrots and wilted spinach for which Eunice paid ingots of gold to some smirking New Age scarecrow at the local farmer's market.

"Is that all there were, Bernard?" Eunice says, observing the small pile of cubes and leaves in the dish after I'd finished.

"Well, once I'd peeled them, carved out worms and slugs, snipped off mottled leaves, got rid of woody stalks and cut out bruises that's all there was. Bring back DDT, that's what I say."

Eunice's face hardened, and she escorted me over to the bin. Flipping the lid up with one Hitler Youth stamp of her fluffy slipper, she showed me the giant heap of peelings and cuttings.

"Now. What's wrong with this?" She picked up out a bent and emaciated carrot with a green tip, and thrust it under my nose.

"It's not ripe, and it's the wrong shape," I retorted.

"What on earth do you mean, 'wrong shape'?"

"A carrot is supposed to be straight. This is a runt, and a disabled one at that. Besides, look at those hairy bits hanging from the end. It's like my mother's chin."

"That is how plants grow. They aren't regiments of orange Tesco soldiers like the ones you would buy, they are individuals, each lovingly immersed in the soil's embracing goodness."

"Anyway," I added. "Once you've peeled it there would be nothing left."

"You're supposed to scrape it, Bernard. All the vitamins are at the surface. These little ones are so tasty," she said. "And what about this?" she said, showing me a discoloured spinach leaf. "I suppose that's not regulation shape either?"

"No, the shape is reasonable, but it's mottled and the stalk is broken and splintered."

"I've told you about this, time and time again," she said, spreading yesterday's (largely unread) *FT* on the kitchen counter. She then tipped the entire bin out onto it, toilet roll centres, pork chop bones, dental floss and greasy grill scrapings included.

"Right," she said. "Start again."

Tuesday 8th May: Hornet's Nest

BAe cannot seem to leave things alone can they? The dropping of the bribery investigation into Saudi dealings last year had already stirred up a hornet's nest in the U.S. with diplomatic notes of protest dropped to Tony Blair. Now, with the proposed $4bn takeover of the biggest maker of armour for Humvees and other vehicles, BAe risks stirring up a hornet's nest in Congress. To me it seems that it doesn't matter that the Pentagon and BAe are best chums, nor does it matter that American defence firms have, over the years, engaged in the level of corruption that makes greasing Saudi palms look like handing out sweets at a kid's party. What matters is that Congressional politicians need only the slightest excuse to champion domestic interests over foreign ones, as happened when they blocked Dubai Ports from buying P&O's leased U.S. port facilities. If only I could persuade, cajole, or fraudulently make my stubborn mother diversify her one-stock BAe shareholding, I could take a dispassionate view. But as things stand I'm hopping mad.

Wednesday 9th May: Preparation H

Last share club meeting before what Harry is calling 'Plan H', the long weekend away for the male members of the club. Harry has briefed us all to arrive early for the meeting so we can sort out the details for the trip before the women arrive. K.P. Sharma popped in early to offer his apologies.

"I'm really sorry, but I can't come on the trip," he said. "Mrs Sharma has put her sandal down. We've got relatives coming over too, and as head of the family I really should be there."

"What about you, Bernard?" Harry asked.

"I'm alright. There just so happens to be a model railway exhibition on at the National Exhibition Centre, so that's a perfect alibi which Eunice will accept. Actually, as we are going past Birmingham, could we stop in there for a half day? I've got shares in Hornby so it could be useful."

"What do we reckon lads?" Harry asked, looking round the table. There was a universal shaking of heads. No anorak hobbies allowed. Such is the lonely life of the railway modeller.

Mike Delaney stubbed out his Lambert & Butler, and exhaled a grey fog. "Actually, I've got a problem too."

"Come on Mike, you'll really enjoy it," Harry said.

It turned out that Mike's other half, Sheila, insisted on coming anywhere that Mike went overnight. "We've never spent a night apart in three decades," Mike said.

"Bloody hell," Harry said. "I've spent most of my married life away from my old tugboat. I like to steam into a few different harbours from time to time. You know, when I was in Cyprus in 1961..."

We eventually shut Harry up before he'd completed the well-worn Sexual Conquest Anecdote 39B, and agreed the times he would pick us up.

"That's just three of us then," Martin said. "Could do with one more to split the petrol money. I am labouring under an insolvency agreement, remember."

"What about the BMW cash?" I reminded him.

"And your Bulgarian wine cellar," Harry added. "Don't think you're going to get away being a skinflint on this trip, sonny boy, because you're not. We're splitting all costs right down the middle."

12.15pm. Chantelle arrived, provoking a quick flurry of hiding maps and brochures. "So what is it you're actually going to do for four days?" she asked.

"It's about reconnecting with the investing basics. We're doing some research, visiting companies, that kind of thing," Harry said with as straight a face as the Rear Admiral could ever manage.

"Which companies? Let's have a look," she said, indicating a piece of paper partially hidden under Harry's elbow. "I might know some."

"Actually, it's not finalised yet," Harry said. The list, it appeared, was hastily scribbled on the back of a final demand from British Gas.

"That sounds really interesting," Chantelle said, pouting a little. "Why aren't we girls invited?"

"It's alright, darling," Harry said. "We can go on our own research weekend later in the year, to Pfizer's Viagra plant in Kent."

"I'd rather chew my own head off," she replied.

"I think there's only room for four of us in Harry's Jag anyway," I said.

"So who's going then?" she asked.

"Me, Harry, Martin," I said "And...um."

"...and Mike," Harry answered. "That's right isn't it, Mike?"

Chantelle, hands on hips stared down at Mike who gently

exhaled another Chernobyl-like gust of tobacco but said nothing. At that moment Cynthia Valkenberg walked in, grimaced at the fug and waved her way through with rapid hand movements. "Jesus, roll on July and freedom to breathe day," she wheezed.

"Cindy," Chantelle said. "Harry's organised a share club weekend away and not invited us."

"Good move guys," said Cynthia. "You'd have to use extraordinary rendition to get me to spend four days in a confined space with that obscene octopus," she said, nodding towards Harry.

Harry repeated his plans for meeting companies, reflecting on investing basics.

"That's not what K.P. said," Chantelle continued. "He said you're planning to get drunk every night, pick up women and behave like a bunch of 16 year-olds."

It was the involuntary grins on all our faces that gave it away.

Chapter Thirteen

The Temple Of Mammon

Friday 11th May: Three Men In A Jag

7.30am. Looking out for Harry, whose car should be outside by now, but isn't. Eunice, padding around in a puce housecoat and slippers now seems to be a little suspicious. "Why is Harry going? I didn't know he even liked train sets."

"Model railways, not train sets. They *aren't* toys." How many million times do I have to correct her? "Harry will be looking at the car exhibition which is in hall three," I lied.

"Oh." Long pause. "And what arrangements have you made to make sure you keep to your low-cholesterol diet?"

"Oh, I'll get by."

"I thought that's what you'd say, Bernard, so I've prepared you some packed lunches." She handed me a Waitrose bag in which were stacked four brick-sized Tupperware boxes.

"Today's lunch is mixed chinese leaf and endive salad with balsamic vinegar, rice crackers and a Yakult yoghurt. Saturday's lunch is a slice of Irmgard's green tea and jasmine flapjack, wholemeal pitta bread, tahini, and a kiwi fruit. For Sunday, there is a pilchard and fennel salad with pine nuts and some of those parsnip crisps that I know you like. For Monday there is a detox bar from the health food shop, and some figs. As a special treat, I've added two squares of bitter black chocolate for each day which can be your elevenses."

Before I could respond, the monologue continued. "Now please, Bernard, you must promise to avoid any stodgy dinners. And try to keep the salads cool. And wrap up well, Birmingham is really quite chilly. I've put that extra long scarf in your bag. Oh and make sure..."

"For God's sake woman, stop fussing. I'm going to Birmingham.

It's not a solo attempt on the summit of K2!"

Finally, Harry pulled up, with Martin next to him, and I was able to escape. I hadn't seen his XJ12 before, and it had a careworn look, with rusty sills peering from beneath the blue paint and the remains of an old hand-painted purple stripe down the side. The back passenger windows were tinted and it had some odd sporty hubcaps.

"Nice motor, Harry," I felt forced to say reaching for the back door handle.

"Not that one, it comes off," Harry warned. "Try the other side. Oh, and dump your luggage in the boot."

I opened the boot to find it almost filled with milk crates loaded with wine bottles. My questions about this were knocked from my mind almost as soon as I'd rounded to the correct door. A gigantic brindled hound was leaning out of the back passenger windows, panting.

"Good Lord! What's that thing?" I said.

"He's not a *thing*, he's Blunkett," said Martin. "He's a bull mastiff cross."

"Crossed with what? King bloody Kong?" I retorted.

The beast panted slowly, its droopy brown eyes watching me as I gently reached under its dripping jaws to the handle.

"Good boy...there, there," I whispered.

"He's alright," Martin said. "He's as soft as butter. Just push him across to the other side."

"Who do you think I am, Geoff Capes?" I responded. "Are we taking him to the vet first or something?"

"No, no," Martin said. "He's coming with us. My brother's paying me £50 a week to look after him while he's in Lanzarote but Holly won't go near him. I thought it's a shame to waste the extra seat, seeing as Mike Delaney isn't coming."

"Is Blunkett paying for his own petrol then?" I said.

"Don't be tight," Martin moaned. "He's an asset. He can guard the car at night."

"But why do I have to sit with him?"

The other two just laughed at that. "Well St. Bernard," said Harry. "You two doggies just have to learn to get along."

At this, Blunkett looked sideways at me as if he'd prefer to be sitting somewhere else too. He sniffed all round my face as I eased the door open. But when I tried to push him, he growled alarmingly, lifting up just a corner of piebald lip so I could see a large tooth.

"Blunkett! Stop that," said Martin. "Make friends!" The dog responded by licking the side of my face, panting noisily into my ear. Finally, I pushed harder, the hound groaned and with a hefty smacking of lips settled itself down on the seat behind Harry and began energetically chewing at his posterior. I slid on to the spit-spattered leather seats, which were already woolly with dog hair.

Harry fiddled under the dashboard, started the engine on the fourth go and we pulled away. Martin got to grips with the stereo and soon the Rolling Stones was hammering through the car, with Blunkett accompanying on the whimper. The full plan was only now explained to me. First we'd drive up to Oxfordshire, to the pretty town of Chipping Norton, where Delia, one of Harry's old flames from his navy days, had a renovated cottage we could stay in for free for a day or two. After that we'd head north to the Yorkshire Dales, which Martin assured me was beautiful, with a choice of fabulous real ales and some good stiff walking, and where he had an appointment with a real master of investment who could teach us all a lot.

"What about all the wine?" I asked. "Are we going to be throwing parties every night?"

"Ah," said Martin, "that's one of my best investments finally coming to fruition." He and Harry laughed as if on some secret.

"So you've finally got a buyer for the Bulgarian stuff?" I asked.

"Not exactly, but once we meet my contact, my oenophile investments will be able to pay dividends."

He refused to tell me any more, so I shrugged and sat back for the ride. With a gradually warming day, the windows open and some very loud music, we pootled along through Tunbridge Wells, East Grinstead and on to Guildford. Harry, a denial of ageing with his grey ponytail protruding beneath a baseball cap and wraparound sunglasses, tapped on the dashboard in time to the music. He was, he explained, avoiding motorways because the XJ12 was two decades old and a little cantankerous. Sure enough, we ground to a halt outside a Jet garage near Haslemere. It was hot and smoky under the bonnet and Harry cursed venomously about the mate who had fixed the car.

"He told me it was running smoothly now. I spent £1,600 with him to put it right and he's just told me a pack of lies."

"Yes, from the heat under there, it is clearly a work of friction," offered Martin. Plugs, points, radiator hose, alternator and various other bits and pieces were checked.

Soon bored by this, I walked into the service station and bought a plain chocolate Bounty, a packet of shortbread biscuits, and something I'd never sampled, a pack of Terry's Chocolate Orange 'Segsations'. By the time I'd got back, Harry had the car running.

Martin, who had been taking Blunkett for a quick walk, ran back to the car, tugging a rather smug looking hound.

"Quick, let's go! Blunkett's done a pile in the doorway of McDonalds and I don't have a bag to clear it up."

We jumped in and Harry screeched away, taking the roundabout at Dukes of Hazzard speed. We went right around twice, before hurtling off towards Farnham, with Blunkett leaning so heavily against me that his drool was dripping down my shirt.

"Take it easy Harry, we've not shot anyone!" I yelled.

"Yeah, but I've seen what Blunkett can leave at the scene of the crime," he retorted.

Friday 11ᵗʰ May: Noon. Berks To Enterprise

With no sign of hot pursuit we eased off on the speed and with the time approaching noon Harry said, "You know, I'm a tad thirsty. What about you, Mr Gale?"

"Ah, Mr Staines, should we happen upon the good fortune of a hostelry, I would be more than happy to imbibe a pint of Throssock's Olde Gutwrencher," Martin said, sinking into giggles. Five minutes later we were the first over the threshold of a thatched pub called The Tethered Goat. Harry sank his first pint in one, and ordered another before I'd had more than a mouthful of mine.

"This should be our first piece of corporate research," Martin said. "An Enterprise Inn, which means it's a property and cash flow play disguised as a pub."

"They've done quite well, haven't they?" I said. "The shares are up fifty per cent since the summer."

"Yeah, maybe so. But there have been loads of complaints by

their pub tenants about the dire contracts they have to work under. Our Camra branch voted to condemn them," Martin added.

"I'm sure that terrified them," I said.

While Harry ordered a pork pie, Martin scanned the menu. "Ye gods, that's expensive! £6.75 for a jacket spud and a sprinkling of cheese, or £9.50 for a chilli! Plus an extra £1.50 if you want sour cream and chives on it," he said.

I peered into the Tupperware box I had concealed under the table. "What about a freshly tossed chinese leaf and endive salad with balsamic vinegar, rice crackers and a Yakult yoghurt, all for £2.50. Does that fit the bill?"

"Where's that?" asked Martin, scanning the menu.

"It's a special," Harry said, with a wink to me.

"What's endive?" Martin asked.

"No idea," I said. "But you can be sure it's good for you."

Finally, I brought the salad up where Martin could see it. "Go on, Martin. Hand tossed, as it were, by my own true love. Yours for two quid."

"I thought you said £2.50?" he asked, peering into the box. "What's the polystyrene packing for? Worried it might break?"

"I'm reliably informed they are rice crackers. Alright. £1.75, final offer."

We finally settled on 75p, which I put towards the baked potato and beans. Martin tipped the salad onto my plate, to disguise its non-Enterprise origins and poked at it with a spare fork. "This endive stuff is really bitter," he said.

"Well, well, a Camra member who doesn't like bitter!" said Harry.

An hour later and £40 lighter we walked back to the Jag. Blunkett had his giant, wet snout pressed to the back window, and his whimpering and groaning could be heard ten yards away.

"Who's had to wait while we eat then?" simpered Martin as he rubbed the dog's gargantuan ears. Blunkett sniffed us in turn, wagging his tail ferociously. "Here boy," said Martin as he sat down, tossing one of the rice crackers to him. I'd never realised the dog could move so fast. It intercepted the cracker like a Patriot missile, jaws smashing it into 1,000 pieces which scattered over the car. The dog then trampled all over me trying to get to the crumbs.

"Nice one, Martin," Harry said. "Those were once real leather seats, you know."

Martin, who'd had two pints, tried to take over the driving from Harry who'd had three and a half. However, in the end I insisted. Not only had I only had one pint, I felt I was owed a break from the heavy breather in the back who'd spent all morning panting into my ear. However, that entailed having Harry show me how to hot-wire the Jag under the dashboard.

"Didn't you have this thing MOT-ed?" I said.

"Nah, MOTs are for wimps."

"How did you get the tax disc then?" I said.

"Take a close look. It's from the old bat's Ford Cellulite."

"But that means you're driving without insurance, in effect."

"Bernard, don't be such an old fart," Harry said. "Next thing you'll be remembering that my ban doesn't actually run out until next month."

"What!"

We then argued for a half hour about whether we should get a hire car, which at least I could legally drive. Martin complained that he couldn't afford his share of that, and Harry didn't want to leave his beloved Jag behind. Finally, I agreed to drive the Jag as far as tonight's stop, and we would get a hire car in the morning.

Once we got going again, the afternoon drifted along nicely. We crossed the Thames at Henley, and let Blunkett off the lead as we ambled along the towpath. Harry picked up a stick, waved it in front of Blunkett's nose and before any of us could stop him, had hurled it into the Thames. The dog gave a baritone bark and tore into the water, swimming out with just his head and the tip of his tail showing.

"Harry," I said. "That was really stupid. Do you realise how long it takes a dog to dry off? And what it smells like while it's happening?"

Blunkett emerged, as dark and drenched as a seal, with stick in mouth and immediately headed for a large family group encumbered with pushchair, pram and picnic. "Doggy!" said a babe in arms, while the women shrieked. Blunkett then decided to shake, subjecting the child and all his living relatives to a shower that would not have disgraced an industrial car wash.

"Oh, for goodness sake," the group's matriarch bellowed at us. "Keep your animal under control."

"Sorry," Martin said cheerily. "He's just a bit boisterous."

Friday 11th May: 6.30pm

Two hours later, with a newly sobered-up Harry at the wheel, we arrived in the vicinity of Chipping Norton. Martin, working from the back of Harry's gas bill for directions, got us lost several times down charming bucolic lanes, between chintzy cottages and red phone boxes. This could have been a pre-war picture, except for the incessant Range Rovers parked in every passing place, across every pavement and up the edge of the village greens, like a herd of metallic rhinos. Trying to escape the sick-bag stench of a hot, wet Blunkett, I stuck my head out of the window and breathed in the Cotswolds' much more attractive aroma: cash!

Finally we left the manicured gardens behind, headed down a farm track behind a pub and pulled up outside a street of semi-detached, 1930s council houses. There was a half full skip at the front, plus numerous scruffy children with trikes, bikes, footballs and even an old Spacehopper. Here at least was a childhood I could relate to. The only car here was a rusty Fiat, minus a wheel. While the kids squealed with delight at the sight of Blunkett, Harry went to the door. It was open, so he went in. Two minutes later he emerged with a stout florid-faced woman in a pinafore.

"That can't be her, can it?" Martin whispered to me. "Look at those wrestler's arms!"

"Harry has catholic tastes," I reminded him.

Delia, it turned out, had been a Wren during Harry's last tour of duty and they had met in Gibraltar. She showed us into the house next door, which had been partially renovated but as yet had no carpet or furniture. It was cool, damp and cluttered with decorating materials but it was, as Harry pointed out, free.

"You can sleep in this room, Martin. Bernard, you'll have the back room with the mattresses," Delia said. "The dog can sleep downstairs in the futility room."

Martin and I looked inquiringly at Harry as Delia walked down the stairs. The grin on his face showed where he was going to sleep. "Her old man walked out a couple of years ago," he whispered, after she had gone. "And there's been nobody since. She'll be like a bloody volcano!"

He opened his overnight bag and fished into a side pocket.

"Look at this," he said. "Here's my most successful investment for a while." He pulled out a pack of tablets and waved it at me. "Now, Bernie me old mate, this is definitely what you need a bit of to deal with Eunice. These are Cialis tablets which I get from a mate who worked at the old Unichem warehouse. You know, part of Alliance-Boots."

"Yes, okay, and now going private. Sorry, Harry, I'm not with you at all," I said.

"Don't be dense. Cialis is like Viagra but better, and it's one of Eli Lilly's most profitable products. Take one of these little fellows, and you'll have a wanger harder than the Angel of the North, and which will last until early closing day." Harry put one of the yellow oval tablets in his mouth and washed it down with a gulp from the bathroom tap. "There. A couple of hours and I'll be able to take on the Shensall Village ladies hockey team."

Half an hour later we were round the corner in the deserted bar of the Woolpack, on a settee with half the stuffing coming out. As I sipped my pint of Old Speckled Hen and munched on a Bounty, I watched motes of dust spinning in the rays of the late afternoon, and thought how peaceful this all was. My reverie (and much else) was disturbed by Delia's appearance. Tottering on high heels and drenched in perfume, she was squeezed into a black and white velvet mini-dress that made her look like a zebra on heat. Harry bought her a double Dubonnet and lemonade while she lit up a cigarette and exhaled in our direction.

"So, boy's weekend away then?" she asked.

"Yeah, bit of a chance to get away from our responsibilities," Martin said, presumably referring to his IVA.

"So what's his wife like, then?" she asked, tipping her head towards Harry, who seemed to be chatting up a young dim-looking barmaid with wide brown eyes and a wet, drooping underlip.

"Avril's very nice," I said. "She puts up with him."

"And the kids have left home haven't they?" she inquired, narrowing her eyes until the mascara threatened to crack.

"Long since," Martin said. In the next three minutes before Harry returned, Delia managed to expertly probe us about the equity value of his house, his pensionable status, and whether he had other cars. She seemed a little disappointed by the answers that Martin, oblivious to her true intent, blurted out.

"But you're all in a share club, I heard."

"That's right. It's not doing that well though. The only one of us with any real money is a woman. From Canada," Martin said.

As Harry rejoined us, Delia elbowed him in the ribs. "And you can take your eyes off her too. She's young enough to be your granddaughter." With that she adjusted her bra strap, displaying an extra acre of quivering cleavage.

Two pints later we returned to the house where Delia served up perhaps the toughest and driest roast beef that I have ever had the misfortune to eat. The yorkshire pudding was like a cowpat and the gravy greasier than Brian Ferry's pillow. Even the carrots had disintegrated. Only then, while Delia was out in the kitchen loudly scraping a pan, did Harry let us know the cruellest irony. The poor woman's surname was Smith, and despite years of effort, she remained a gastronomic rebuke to her more famous namesake.

By 10pm, back at the Woolpack, and three more pints of Speckled Hen later, the evening was becoming surreal. Delia was sprawled on Harry's lap, whispering and giggling into his ear. Oblivious, Martin was droning on about the attractions of the Pennine Way. Delia wasn't having any of it.

"I don't like the Pennine Way. That position always gave me cramp," she giggled. "I prefer Howard's Way. Besides, with Howard's Way there's always repeats. And I like repeats, don't I Harry?"

Harry used the laughter as cover to readjust his trousers for about the hundredth time, hand in pocket.

"Whoops, what was that?" giggled Delia.

Time to retire, I reckoned and headed off to my thin mattress and copious supply of confectionery.

Saturday 12ᵗʰ May: In Delia Smith's Kitchen

4am. Awoke with awful thumping headache. However, the thumping wasn't confined to my head as the tap-tap-tap of a headboard on the party wall revealed. Got up, lurched into the bathroom and was sick. Fell back to sleep, but awoke again two hours later to the same refrain. In the next room, heard Martin snoring, so crept downstairs to watch the dawn break. Had completely forgotten about Blunkett, who came panting out to greet me and began whining for food.

8.30am. Went next door and shared a coffee with a dishevelled Delia, who was wearing an obscenely short bathrobe. Harry, she told me, was in a dead sleep. "Well, almost all of him," she added, with a mischievous giggle. Rather than inquire after the exceptions, I offered to wash up last night's dishes. This turned out to be a more strenuous activity than normal, much of it requiring hammer and chisel rather than a gentle application of suds. Between vigorous sessions with the Brillo, she told me the poignant tale of her abandonment, her financial struggle to bring up three children on income support and housing benefit, and now that they too had left home, her loneliness. Completely unexpectedly, she turned, put her arms around me and began to cry on my shoulder.

"Is that how your life is too?" she asked, sunken and make-up streaked eyes looking into mine. "A complete wreck?"

"No, no, not at all," I said, examining the mascara streaks just deposited on my shirt. "I'm very lucky. Eunice and I are well-suited." This statement was perhaps less out of loyalty than a determination not to bond further with this promiscuous panda. Who knows where further encouragement would lead?

Martin arrived shortly, and after a big mug of Delia's tea (milk on the turn, not-quite-boiling water) we were offered a cooked breakfast. Cereal and toast would have been wiser, but after a skin full of Old Speckled Hen only a fry-up will do. So while we waited for Harry to emerge, Delia deep-fried half a dozen Morrison economy bangers (which spat then exploded), immolated six rashers of streaky bacon (shattered on fork impact), and drowned three eggs (the rubbery mess entangled in a crazy paving of broken shell). The fried bread was like the bilge rag of the Amoco Cadiz, while the black pudding had fossilized into clinker. While Martin and I fought for toast and marmalade to ease down this charnel house breakfast, Delia chattered about her kids, and her ex, Stanley. Soon afterwards, Delia disappeared upstairs for another energetic hour with the headboard. Poor Harry!

11.30am. Martin took Blunkett for a two mile walk. Delia now down and fully dressed. Harry had still not emerged. Went up with a cup of Delia's 'tea' to see if he was ready to rejoin the land of the living (until the first poisonous sip, of course), but was unprepared for the sight I beheld. Harry was still snoring, the centrepiece of a jumble sale of discarded clothing, greying pillows and the rank odour of human sweat. With my gorge rising, I left the tea on the window ledge and fled.

It took until 3pm for Harry to surface, and he looked like death.

Naturally, Martin and I were killing ourselves laughing especially when we noticed the careful way he stood or sat.

"Feeling a little stiff today?" I asked.

"Alright, alright, shut up," Harry moaned. "I've got a bloody blister. It's agony, but it still won't go down."

We then decided that you definitely could have too much of a good thing.

Saturday 12th May (again): On The Road By 3.30pm

Waved goodbye to Delia, as she blew us kisses. Drove into Chipping Norton, desperate for proper food. As if by magic, Kebab Heaven was just opening. As we sat on the bench outside, gorging on crisp pitta bread full of donna meat, garlic sauce and shredded lettuce, we all agreed this little eatery knocked spots off poor Delia Smith's kitchen.

Jag controversy resumed. I wanted to hire a car that was road legal, but Harry wouldn't leave his previous Jag behind and Martin balked at any extra expense. Outvoted, I at least got to drive seeing as Harry was in no fit state. While I tried my hand at the hot-wiring technique, I saw that we were almost out of fuel, despite having filled up in East Grinstead.

"Er, Harry. Just how thirsty is this beastie?" I asked.

"About nine or ten to the gallon," he responded diffidently.

"What!" yelled Martin, knowing that it was his turn next to buy fuel. "It's going to cost us hundreds just to get to Swaledale."

"Nah," said Harry.

"Oh yes it is," Martin said, pressing buttons on his Korean watch/calculator. Look, say 90p a litre, that's about £4.50 a gallon. It's about 200 miles to Swaledale, so that's twenty gallons at best, £90 each way."

"Time to buy shares in BP then," Harry said.

"Or better get a small hire car," I suggested.

"And where would we put him in a Nissan Micra?" Martin pointed to Blunkett, whose monstrous head was resting ruminatively on the passenger headrest. His big sad eyes seemed hurt by the accusation as he looked at each of us in turn. His ears sagged gradually.

"Well, perhaps he'd agree to pull it," I responded.

Saturday 12th May (yet again): Yorkshire Dales At Midnight

Saturday night turned into Sunday morning as we passed Catterick Camp and turned towards Richmond. Martin and I took turns driving as Harry and Blunkett slept together in a tangled drooling heap on the back seat. The day's fine weather had dissolved into a cool and windy evening where rags of clouds as livid as bruises were stretched across a subdued sunset. Beyond Richmond, the austere beauty of Swaledale emerged in a craggy silhouette. I stopped the car by a damp, fragrant meadow near a long, narrow stone bridge. Blunkett whined to be let out, so I gave him free rein on the field, only sure of his location by the frenetic panting. Martin came and leaned next to me on the gate. "This is what I wanted to come up for. I miss all this now I'm in the south. Tomorrow we can all do a good long hike."

Martin had arranged for us to stay in a mate's caravan in the village of Reeth. We pulled up outside Charlie's farm and he showed us to the caravan, which was a chilly, shabby and mildewed affair around the back under some apple trees. While the facilities were basic, the food was tremendous. Charlie's wife Sue had prepared a game stew which had simmered for hours awaiting our arrival, and was none the worse for that. Thick doorsteps of local brown bread soaked up the gravy. Half an hour later, we were all nodding off. Harry, who had barely said a word all day, was tipped into one bed at the back, while Martin and I crept into separate mattressed alcoves. Above the low roar of the gas-bottle heater I could hear the sound of the nearby stream jostling river-bed stones, and the occasional hoot of an owl.

Sunday 13th May: Woken By Waterfalls

Awoke at 6am to the sound of Harry pissing prodigiously from the open door of the caravan, and his ensuing sigh of relief. Seeing I was awake he said: "That's the first time in 24 hours I haven't had to do a handstand when I wanted a pee."

"Serves you right," I said turning over. But now sleep was impossible as Harry trundled around the caravan, whistling, farting (plus giving himself marks out of ten) and opening cupboards.

Breakfast was mushrooms and bacon on toast with grilled local bacon and greenhouse tomatoes. I offered a Terry's Orange Segsation each as afters. Delicious. Then it was down to the walking. Now I've never been much of a walker, but there's quite a contrast between sauntering down to the local shops in the drizzle, and striding across magnificent moorland on a fine spring day.

"So when are we meeting this investment guru then?" I asked Martin as we crossed a ladder-style over a drystone wall.

"Later today in Richmond. You won't be disappointed."

Four miles later I was beginning to flag. Harry, too, looked pained and complained incessantly about his blister every time we crossed a stile, but all he earned was laughter. His walk, normally ramrod straight had gradually become to resemble that of Richard III. Martin, though, was in his element, pointing out local landmarks and explaining the local economy. After another two hours, I'd definitely had enough. Rain clouds were approaching, and we looked to have another mile or more of boggy plodding before any chance of descent.

"It's really hurting now," said Harry. "You have no idea."

"Well, you've been doing your best to tell us," I responded.

"Isn't this wonderful," Martin said holding out his arms to the enfolding vista of towering purple clouds. The wind picked up and the first drops of rain had us digging in our packs for waterproofs. Martin was perfectly prepared with the latest breathable fabrics, including gaiters, while I had a flat cap and a Barbour jacket. Harry's preparations were even more basic, not much more than a yellow pac-a-mac and a pink pom-pom hat. The ferocity of the rain was appalling, driven sideways with a gusty wind and seeping in down necks and up sleeves. We sought refuge behind the lichen-scarred walls of an old sheep pen, from which two ragged old ewes eyed us suspiciously. Harry then dug under his soggy clothing and produced a hip flask from which he swigged enthusiastically before passing it around. "Ten year old Islay. Don't say I never do anything for you two!"

The smoky, burning liquid drew heat through our throats and gave us renewed energy to press on, where Reeth was now beckoning through gaps in the low-hanging cloud. By ten past six, we were in the bar at The Black Bull, enjoying pints of Old Peculier in front of an open fire.

Sunday 13th May (evening): The Temple Of Mammon

At half past seven we headed off slowly on the winding road back to Richmond, with Martin driving. He parked in the cobbled market square, and with instructions in hand walked up a street fronted with traditional shops. Between two shop frontages was a rough latched door, leading to a brick passageway through the building to unkempt gardens and a row of tumbledown privies beyond. A gated metal fire escape wound up to the floor above us. Martin pressed a bell on the gate and a head emerged from the window above. We climbed the stairs and were shown into an untidy and smoky kitchen.

"I'm Timothy Burnside," said a fat, bald man whose ruddy face and bulging eyes made him look like he was about to lose his temper. He greeted Martin warmly, and listened carefully as Martin introduced the rest of us.

"So you lads are all big investors then?" he asked, pouring us mugs of strong tea from a teapot with a cosy on.

"Well, none of us is exactly in the George Soros league," I said. For some reason he found this hugely funny.

"Look. We've got a way with money up 'ere," he said puffing on his pipe. "Do nowt too hasty and nowt that relies on unproven promises. I've been investing for 45 years and I never lose. I just watch what other people are getting excited about and pouring money into, and I go the other way. Contrarian yes, but more'n that."

"What are your top picks then?" I asked.

"Same as they always are. Incumbent providers who cannot be displaced. Big annoying buggers like banks, water and electric companies. Even BT, which has you paying ten quid a month for a bit of fifty-year-old wire into your 'ouse that no-one else will ever own. We all 'ate 'em, but we can't displace the buggers and they almost all pay good dividends."

There were general nods of assent before Timothy continued. "D'you know what my best-ever investment was, eh?" He looked at each of us in turn. "I'll tell yer. It made me £100 for every £1 what I invested. Any ideas? Well I'll tell you what it wasn't. No bloody biotech bollocks, no technology tosh, no fancy emerging market rubbish, nothing like that."

"Go on, put us out of our misery," said Harry.

"It were docks, and the land around them. Associated British Ports shares, which I bought on Valentine's Day 1983, when they were privatised for 14p each and sold at 950p when they were taken over in 2006. With all the dividends re-invested over all them years I made over a hundred and fifty grand on that one share."

"But how did you know it would do so well?" I asked.

"It's quite simple. Mrs Thatcher hated docks and she hated dockers. Couldn't get shot of the lot fast enough. Strikes, bad management and a very dull business. It was priced to go, that's for sure. Far too cheap. But I could see that there was loads of land in these places, land which could be sold to distribution firms, for warehouses, all sorts. You see, you can't displace a harbour or a dockside. It's a unique and permanent asset, as is an airport. They may be dull but they usually make cash hand over bloody fist."

Harry and I looked at each other, and the cracked tiles and stained ceiling in the flat. "So Timothy, didn't you ever fancy buying yourself a big house," Harry asked.

"I did. Enormous rectory it was, plus 14 acres with fabulous views. Bloody missus has got it now…This is now my Temple of Mammon."

"Let's get down to business then," Martin said, leading us back to the car. Delving into the Jaguar's boot I then realised that the five milk crates were actually loaded with empty wine bottles, with corks roughly pushed back in.

"What's all this about then, Martin," I asked. "Are you investing in bottle banks?"

"You'll see," he said. We lugged the crates up the metal staircase back into Tim's kitchen, rather glad at this point they weren't full.

"Have you got all the corks?" Tim asked, as we set the crates on the floor.

"Most of them," Martin replied. Though some don't match completely, you'd have to look closely to notice."

Tim held one bottle, a fine-looking Saint-Estèphe, up under Martin's nose. "I'm not paying for that one you daft bugger. Look, there's a bloody wine trail across the label. I thought you'd checked 'em."

"Oh, right," Martin said. "That must have slipped through."

It took a further half an hour for Tim to pick his way through the bottles, muttering and grunting. He then picked out each cork, checked it for signs of damage and after tossing away a good quarter of them, nodded that he was done. He stuck his hand in his pocket and produced a roll of cash. "There you go. That's your share," he said, tucking it into Martin's top pocket.

"What IS going on?" I hissed, into Martin's ear.

Harry guided me away, and down the stairs. "Bernie, don't go all legit on us on this one, eh? It's just a little something to help Martin through his financial difficulty."

Finally, back in the car, Martin let on what he was up to.

"You know that street of nobby restaurants off the London Road? Well, I went to each of them, showed them my old Oxfam badge, saying that we needed to collect empty wine bottles which would be crushed and used for building materials in African villages. The corks, I said would be re-processed to make light and effective roofing material. Seeing as they have to pay to get the glass taken away, those Michelin-starred eateries couldn't help me fast enough. In just two months, I filled the garage and shed. Most of it was rubbish, but with the help of a book I borrowed off Tim I was able to narrow it down to the best five per cent of Bordeauxs that are suitable for laying down."

"I'm sorry," I said. "Call me dense, but I still don't see why African villagers couldn't get by with any old plonk bottle?" At this point, Harry started giggling and shaking his head.

"No, Bernard. Look," said Martin. "Forget Africa, that was just the excuse. Tim runs an engineering firm, and he has acquired a second-hand bottling and foil-top machine which can re-seal bottles using the original cork, so long as it's not too damaged. Once he has refilled these Bordeaux vintage bottles from boxes of cheap wine, Tim can resell them for a 2,000 per cent profit."

"But isn't it obvious the moment you drink some?" I asked.

"It might be, but Tim is marketing these as mixed cases of wine to lay down for at least ten years. By the time anyone realises it's Kwik Save's Libyan foot-washing wine, it will be far too late to do anything about it. Besides, as he told me, a lot of wine that has been properly laid down will still spoil. It's just a chance you take. It's priced to attract the wannabe collectors, not the professional buyers you get at auctions. I've got three hundred and fifty quid that says this works!" he said gleefully, waving his wodge of cash.

"Martin, you're nothing but a fraudster!" I said. "This is quite wrong and I won't be any part of it."

"You already are a part of it, mate," Harry said.

"In which case, put a chunk of that towards the petrol," I said, pointing at Martin's wodge of notes.

"No, we've got a better idea," Harry said. It was a day later before I discovered what that was.

Monday 14th May: Making Hay

After another night in the caravan, and after saying our goodbyes to Charlie and Sue, we headed back down the A1. Harry drove, while Blunkett leaned all over me in the back, panting. I suspected I was beginning to smell of dog. When we approached Leeds, Harry turned off. It wasn't, as I had thought, for petrol. My questions were answered with "wait and see". I began to feel a little nervous as we approached the depressing terraced houses of Chapeltown. This I recalled as the Yorkshire Ripper's stamping ground, not anywhere I would really like to be. Martin navigated us into a street of imposing and substantial Victorian houses, of the type a dental practice might occupy. Finally, we stopped at one whose frontage was obscured by large laurel bushes. It was exactly noon.

"OK Bernard," Harry said. "Would you just ring the bell there and say Harry sent you? We'll be back in two hours."

"I think I'd rather stay here…"

"No you wouldn't, go on in."

"No, I'm not sure what you're up to…"

"For God's sake Bernard, we've had a whip round to pay for you." Harry and Martin gradually eased me out and watched as I walked sheepishly up to the front door. My hand hesitated over the bell, and I looked around at Harry and Martin, who were nodding and waving me on. After dithering for a minute, I heard a noise and the door was opened from the inside.

"Well, Bernard are you going to wait there all day?" Facing me was a very attractive woman, about 30, and of my own height, with shoulder-length dark hair and bright blue eyes. She was dressed in a tight but smart suit that emphasised her hourglass figure. With a practised hand she reached out and grabbed my belt buckle, firmly pulling me into the house. It was indeed like an upmarket dentist's reception area, tastefully furnished with expensive furniture and carpets. She shut the door, and motioned me to sit while she checked in what looked like a visitor's book.

As I sank into a soft sofa I said, "Look, I'm terribly sorry but how do you know my…"

"Be quiet, Bernard," she said, walking up to me. "There's no need to be nervous. Everything's been arranged."

"What's been…?"

"Don't interrupt. Speak only when you're spoken to," she said, looking down at me, hands on hips. "These are the rules. If you want to speak, you must say 'please Mistress Sadie'. Then, perhaps, I will give you permission. Is that understood?"

Oh my God. This was worse than I feared.

"Yes…er, Mistress, look…"

"Go upstairs. First door on the right. Undress completely, shower thoroughly and wait for me."

"Actually, I'm terribly sorry…er Mistress…but I think there's been an awful mistake. To be honest, this isn't my kind of thing…"

The woman seized my jaw sharply in one very firm hand and pushed me back on the sofa, her handsome face very close to mine.

"Deep down, all men want and enjoy what I have to offer. I am the best in the business, and I know what you need. Do you want to risk insulting me? That would be very, very dangerous."

"No, of course not...it's just."

"Do you want to be punished?"

"Of course not."

"Then do as I say IMMEDIATELY."

Reluctantly, I went upstairs, entered the room and closed the door. The room was spacious and neatly furnished like an upmarket hotel room. However, any remaining sense of normality was soon swept away by what I saw next. Rather than a bed, there was a large and sturdy wooden table in the centre of the room with a set of leather cuffs with buckles at each corner. One wall was decorated with a large framed black and white photograph of Mistress Sadie in a leather catsuit and thigh boots, one heel resting on the prone form of some agonised and bound male figure. In her hand she brandished what looked like (from vague memories of Boy's Own adventure stories) a cat o'nine tails. My heart started to beat wildly. I had to escape, but how? With my clothes still fully on, I rushed to the en-suite and turned on the shower, then went over to the bedroom window. Pulling the drawn curtains apart I looked down on an unkempt garden, with a broken swing, an old greenhouse, a broken-down fence and an alleyway running along behind. I slid up the sash and poked my head through. To my left was an old lead drainpipe, the only possible way of descending without breaking my neck. I lifted the window as high as it would go and straddled the window sill. Gingerly I reached out for the drainpipe, trying to secure a good grip. It was a bit of stretch, but the noise of a door opening in the room behind me gave me the courage I needed. I leapt out and grabbed the pipe, my brogues scrabbling to get some kind of grip. With a horrifying squeal of shoe soles, I slid for a good ten feet before leaping onto the grass. I landed badly, banging my head on the rusty frame of the swing and fell on my back. Above me at the window was Mistress Sadie. And she was laughing fit to burst.

I think I'm going to kill Harry when I see him.

Monday 14th May: Evening Shift

3pm. Harry had been expecting me to be unable to sit down, but he was a little surprised on seeing my return to the waiting Jaguar that Mistress Sadie had instead given me a limp like Long John Silver and a large bruise on the back of the head.

"So did you enjoy it?" Martin asked eagerly.

"It was truly an unforgettable experience," I replied truthfully.

Once Harry heard what had actually happened he looked heavenwards and swore. "Jesus, Bernard. What a waste. That cost a hundred and fifty nicker, and that was at a discount because Sadie's me sister-in-law's niece."

"Good grief, I can't believe you would have invested so much in a practical joke."

"It wasn't just me, matey. We had thirty quid from Mike Delaney, and a tenner from Chantelle..."

"Chantelle! I won't be able to look her in the face...how dare you!"

"She thought it was a hilarious idea. She's convinced you would love to be thrashed."

"Even K.P. put in a fiver," nodded Martin.

"I don't believe it..."

"Yeah, of course we said it was for a personal training course," Harry said, sniggering.

"Well. I think you've all been completely irresponsible," I said.

"Listen mate," said Harry. "I can't think of anyone who is as repressed as you. You just need to relax and let life take its course. Anyway, needless to say, there won't be a word to Eunice so long as you keep schtum about the wine investments…"

Ah. Blackmail. Now I get it.

Chapter Fourteen

Bull In A China Shop

Tuesday 15th May: Shanghai, Sell Low

Breakfast. Choke on my toast and Frank Cooper's marmalade as I read that the Swiss (of all people) are now to investigate BAe on charges of money laundering. The very nation which rakes in hundreds of millions in banking fees from the world's organised crime bosses through its wonderful banking secrecy, has the nerve to pour salt into the wounds of the Jones family inheritance. What *am* I going to do to get my mother to sell those damn shares?

Elevenses: Have secretly reneged on my agreement not to store comestibles in the Hornby drawer. Have six Cadbury Mini Rolls there, which fit perfectly within the box which contained my Hornby double-O breakdown crane. Must remember to carefully dispose of the wrappers before the next cholesterol gestapo patrol.

Peter Edgington rings to say the whole family is off today on a giant railway excursion from Moscow to Vladivostok, followed by a luxury two-month trip through China. Perfect Peter has, as usual, exercised his 'sell in May' routine, paring his portfolio to a minimum ahead of the summer. He takes delight in announcing that the whole gargantuan expedition will be covered by dividend payments received in the first week of May. While I tried to stop my lip curling Huw Edwards-style, Peter then gave his market view.

"Watch out for Shanghai, Bernard," he said. "I think it's the bubble that is going to put paid to our four-year bull market. I wouldn't be surprised if it goes pop before we get back in September. And don't opt for gilts either. Inflation is going to do them some damage. Stay in cash."

Monday 21st May: Dot Beyond Infinity

Visit Dot, hoping to find some paperwork relating to her e-mail account. If I can find and access her e-mail, I can request another password from her broker and access her account. Then I will diversify that single, infuriating shareholding in BAe. While she's in the kitchen making tea, I quickly rifle through her letter rack and see, horror of horrors, all sorts of charitable begging letters. Cat protection, abandoned dogs, demented donkeys and sundry other societies, using doe-eyed creatures to lure her into making a bequest. Knowing my mother, she'll change her will to leave £200,000 to a refuge for cross-eyed marmosets in Knutsford and just £20 to her long-suffering family. Find nothing, absolutely nothing relating to e-mail. On her return however, notice she is wearing some peculiar and outsize footwear. Below the support bandages and varicose veins sit a pair of golden training shoes, adorned with the logo *Performance Beyond Infinity* and the signature of the Canadian sprinter Ben Johnson. My nonagenarian mother, who couldn't spring out of an armchair in 9.87 seconds, seems unaware of their indicated purpose.

"What's your best time for the 100 metres then, Mum?" I ask.

"What's that?"

"The shoes. You know they're for athletes?"

"Don't be silly. They were in the £5.99 bin at Shoefayre. Reduced because they didn't have any more gold laces. Ooh, but they're ever so comfy. Got plenty of room for me corn plasters."

Perhaps it isn't so silly after all. It turns out there is a charity tea at the community centre this afternoon, with rumours of smoked salmon circulating among the clattering classes. After the fiasco at the Val Doonican tribute concert, Dot has been banned from bringing Maurice, her mobility vehicle. So with sprinter's shoes, she is perhaps preparing for a personal best in the sandwich grab. Just so long as she doesn't get tested for Lemsip or other performance-enhancing substances.

Wednesday 23rd May: Mince Pie Fight

Share club at the Ring o'Bells. Harry Staines is seeking enlightenment about the war of words which has just broken out between Inter Link Foods, the heavily indebted food firm that he has the misfortune to own shares in, and potential bidder McCambridge Group. The latter has threatened to withdraw unless it receives more cooperation.

"I can't understand why Inter Link won't let them talk to their bankers," he says, lamenting the fall of five per cent in the shares that this spat has caused.

"I'd let them talk to mine," says Martin Gale, whose IVA is still causing him distress. "I'll happily let them buy me out."

K.P. Sharma, lifts his head from a copy of the *Times*. "Martin, when the first bidder approaches you, then I know that the takeover boom must be nearing its end. All debt, no equity, and ripe for a change of management," he chuckled.

"Martin is a cash shell without the cash," suggested Harry.

Martin's protestations at these slanders are drowned by laughter. Then K.P. Sharma turns to me.

"What price did you sell Tanfield at last month?" he asks.

"About 103p," I replied wearily, knowing what will come next.

"Did you know it's now over 150p?" he said, innocently.

Oh, how they adore twisting the knife!

Friday 25th May: Life In The Gulag

At breakfast, Eunice is seen chuckling away over something in the *Daily Mail*. As I lower the *Telegraph*, she eyes me briefly and continues sniggering as she reads. "Good old Beverley Charman," she says. "You take him to the cleaners, dear."

The £48m divorce settlement accorded this woman by the courts has clearly stimulated my wife to some unaccustomed morning jollity. After a brief harrumph, I return to the litany of woe in the share price columns: Spirent (which has doubled since I sold it at 37p a year ago), Tanfield (up 25 per cent in a month since I sold), and of course, BAe, 442p, down 20p in the last few weeks, another ebbing of the Jones family fortune.

"Bernard," says Eunice, brightly. "How much are we worth?"

"We?" I say. "You mean the house I bought with *my* MoD salary, the share portfolio funded from *my* savings, and the two cars bought with *my* money?"

"Oh, really. Against that you need to account for the value of the loss of the best years of my life, the agony of bearing two children, by breech, which as we know is from your side of the family, decades of ironing, putting up with that useless Electrolux when you wouldn't buy me a Dyson, scrubbing floors..."

"What do you mean scrubbing floors? You've never scrubbed a floor in your life! The only time you've ever been on your knees in this house is with a magnifying glass to look for incriminating biscuit crumbs in the den. Let's face facts. I've given you four decades of comfortable middle class life. You make it sound like a chapter in the *Gulag Archipelago*."

"If I do divorce you, Bernard, I will make it sound a lot worse than that, believe me. And I'll be going for 75 per cent, not 50. You'll be lucky to get visiting rights to the model railway."

Wednesday 30ᵗʰ May: Mixed Meat Curry

K.P. Sharma bounces into the Ring o'Bells for share club, delighted by the story of the sale of family-owned curry sauce business Patak's for a rumoured £150m to Associated British Foods. "This is true British entrepreneurship," he says. "A Kenyan Indian couple arrive in the U.K. with just five pounds in 1957, start making samosas on the kitchen table, and now look at them."

Mike Delaney, the club's own curry fanatic agrees. "Before them, curry sauces were so weak you could hardly taste them. It was all corn flour and additives, and no flavour. Patak's changed all that. My missus can now make a lamb rogan josh almost as good as the Koh-I-Noor and at half the price."

"Then should we buy some AB Foods shares for the club?" says Martin Gale, tucking into a packet of Scampi Fries.

"Hold on," says K.P. "AB Foods has been wooing the family for five years. If they have decided to sell now, that looks like the top of the market. I'm not sure we should be buying. Besides, Patak's will only be a small part of AB Foods. It has a big sugar business and the fashion retailer Primark."

Chantelle, in lime green flying suit, engineer's boots and orange gelled hair, nods in agreement. "Primark's a hot ticket these days, it's got some pretty good clothes."

"I take it you don't shop there then," Harry says, eyeing Chantelle's eclectic ensemble.

The rest of us smile nervously while Chantelle approaches, sticks her tongue out at Harry (revolting piercing all-too-visible) and empties her bag of peanuts into his pint of Spitfire.

Saturday 2nd June: A Tissue Of Lies

10am. Summoned from a blissful railway reverie in the loft by Eunice's shouting. It seems that a tissue has disintegrated in the dark wash, coating a full load of laundry with fragments. It is, needless to say, my fault. "Bernard, I've told you time and time again to check your trouser pockets," she says.

"Could it perhaps have been you?" I have the temerity to ask.

"Of course not." She then shows me the offending pair of corduroys, inverts a pocket and reveals ribbons of damp tissue.

"Planted evidence, clearly," I say. "Besides, if you hadn't decreed in 1971 or whenever that you would never wash another dirty cotton hanky, we wouldn't be in this mess today."

14.57pm. Finally finished my community sentence, just short of five hours. Eunice issued me with tweezers to clear the entire load of laundry of tiny fragments of tissue. Have agonising cramp in my right hand after de-linting no less than 37 pairs of Eunice's industrial-sized bloomers, a combined surface area surely exceeding Hyde Park. No wonder the panty looms of China's textile heartland are never silent. The groaning knicker drawers of Britain's womenfolk must be the biggest contribution to that country's staggering economic growth.

Chapter Fifteen

Earnings Guidance

Wednesday 6th June: Beyoncé All Limits

Share club meeting at the Ring o'Bells. Cynthia Valkenberg makes an appearance for the first time in a month, and in brisk mood sets about reviewing our investments. Since she took charge, we've made 2.5 per cent in six weeks, while the FTSE has been flat overall. She's made a packet on BSkyB, a bit on BT, and lost on Debt Free Direct and Oakdene Homes. Even our own original pre-Cynthia investment, BHP Billiton, is now firmly in profit. Of course 90 per cent of everything that has been made is her money.

"You see, guys," she says. "What you need is a little female guidance and some self discipline. Cut down on the booze, concentrate and it'll all turn out fine. Harry, did you finish reading that point and figure charting book I gave you?"

Harry is looking over Cynthia's shoulder, hypnotised by the TV in the main bar, where Beyoncé is grinding out her latest number dressed, apparently, in only a J-cloth and some cling film.

"Earth calling Harry," Cynthia croons. "Hello?"

"Sorry, just checking on our best investment, Sky, to see that the standard of the product has been maintained," Harry murmurs.

"That reminds me guys," Cynthia said. "We really, really need a better venue for the meetings."

At this there are groans, loudest from Chantelle, who often combines bar duties with her club membership. "C'mon," says Cynthia. "This place is disgusting. It's dirty, noisy and smoky."

K.P. Sharma nods vigorously in agreement.

"Only smoky for another three weeks," Mike Delaney reminds her, from within his personal Lambert & Butler halo.

"And it's free," adds Martin Gale, who I now recall hasn't

coughed up for a round since my birthday.

"Look. Let's hold the next meeting at my place," Cynthia says. "We'll lay on a spread and even get you some beers in."

We readily agree, mainly out of nosiness to see inside the famed Manor House at Old Dorringsfield, and meet her hubby.

Thursday 7ᵗʰ June: Not So Chuffed

Notice that Hornby shares, having done so well for so long, have fallen in the wake of last week's disappointing results. Adverse currency movements are part of the problem but perhaps brokers were over-optimistic in their expectations. Slightly tempted to expand my miniscule holding of 200 at these lower prices and in what is after all a year of recovery and transition, but *Chronic Investor* says the shares are fairly valued. Perhaps I'll just wait. I wonder if Peter Edgington still has his 20,000 Hornby shares. If so, he can't have made too much because he only bought at around 230p, and that's only 20p below the current price. It's nice to know that however poorly my own shares perform, I can take some wicked pleasure in the portfolio imperfections of Perfect Peter.

Elevenses: Spilled an entire cup of coffee on *Railway Modeller* magazine before I'd had chance to read a single article. Damn.

Saturday 9ᵗʰ June: Bernard, Like Nature, Abhors A Vacuum

Just got the BT bill, and they are now charging me £4.50 for the privilege of paying by cheque! Absolutely fuming, phoned them up to give them a piece of my mind, and after going through voice mail hell ("Press one to vent your spleen about BT Together option one, press two to bellow at a customer services representative at our call centre in Uranus or press three to be held in an endless loop while paying local call charges") ended up in a queue listening to Mozart's Divertimento in D, endlessly repeated until my brain reached the temperature of a Chernobyl reactor.

Elevenses: Two illicit Cadbury's Mini Rolls from the Hornby drawer, while Eunice clattered about upstairs doing housework. Just as I prepared to bite into the second one Eunice burst in to the den, vacuum cleaner akimbo.

"Aha! Caught in the act," she hissed, pointing the extended nozzle of the Electrolux at me like some assegai-wielding Amazon. "I thought we had an agreement. Now you are going to regret it."

At a click of her heel, the machine roared into life. Advancing steadily, she waved the nozzle towards my face while I took a gigantic Cadbury chomp. I grabbed Prescott, the giant suede pig, from on top of the PC and used him as a shield in an attempt to defend myself against this unprovoked assault into the sovereign territory of Lemon Curdistan.

"Don't forget I took fencing lessons when I was at St Cecilia's," Eunice trumpeted. With a quick feint to the groin, she lured my Prescott parrying arm down, and then stabbed at my right hand. With a gigantic slurp the remaining half of my Mini Roll disappeared into its greedy maw.

"Now," she said, changing the nozzle to the hyper-suction one (for 'hard to reach crevices'), "I'm going in search of the Mini Roll that got away. Open wide, Bernard!"

Monday 11ᵗʰ June: Woolf At The Door

Lord Justice Woolf has been asked by BAe Systems to head a new ethics committee to oversee how the company conducts its affairs. This looks like a clever ploy to keep the Americans happy. He apparently won't be looking into the past, where the real Al Yamamah dirt is, but will oversee the future. Still, I'm not sure that maverick members of Congress will be happy to nod through BAe's $4.1bn takeover of Armor Holdings without creating a fuss. There's a nasty whiff about BAe, and this does nothing to dispel it. While our family is decidedly long on BAe shares, and I can do nothing about it yet, this is enough reason to feel nervous.

Tuesday 12ᵗʰ June: Pharmaceutical Glut

Woke up with awful low back pain. Probably related to trying to reach under the desk yesterday to retrieve an incriminating Mini Roll wrapper. Tottered into the bathroom looking for painkillers, while Eunice yelled directions at me from the comfort of bed.

"Use that ibuprofen gel, Bernard."

"Can't see it in the drawer. Do we have any?"

"Yes, of course, in the cupboard."

"In the kitchen?"

"No, no, in the BATHROOM. Why would I keep it in the kitchen? I'm not going to cook with it, Bernard, am I?"

"Well, I can't find it. Ah, you don't mean in the bathroom cabinet do you? With the mirrors on?"

"Yes, cabinet, that's what I said. Don't you listen?"

So I yank open the cabinet door, releasing an avalanche of tubes of ointments, salves and creams. As I sort through the heap on the floor I find cures for everything from conjunctivitis to something called thrush. (Perhaps I better let the Man from U.N.C.L.E know.) What I can't find is anything to deal with back pain.

"It's not here," I say.

"Yes it IS, oh for God's sake." The thundering of not so tiny feet indicates Eunice's arrival. "Look, THERE it is," she says, having instantly located it. What is it with women, do they have bloody radar or something?

As I look through this vast array of potions, a history of billions invested by Merck, Pfizer, GlaxoSmithKline and others, I notice that almost every product, even the Listerine, is out of date. If every household in the land does what we do, no wonder the drug sector has hard such a sharp de-rating.

Wednesday 13ᵗʰ June: To The Manor Born

Share club meeting at the Manor House at Old Dorringsfield, Cynthia's home. Behind the beech hedge, and two acres of grounds, it's even grander than I thought. As Mike Delaney drove us up the gravel drive, Harry, Martin and I gaped at the mullioned windows, the croquet lawn and the indoor swimming pool visible through the Victorian style conservatory.

"Good grief, she's loaded," Martin whimpered.

Cynthia meets us at the door, wearing leather trousers and a bolero style top. We are shown into a giant sun lounge, all colonial furniture and palms, while she gets some drinks. The drinks arrive: bottled Young's bitter for Harry and Martin, cider and blackcurrant for Chantelle, and a G&T for me. K.P. Sharma sticks to mineral water. Cynthia ushers us into the dining room where a blonde fortyish woman is laying out food.

"Blimey, outside caterers, the works," whispers Martin as he takes in the sumptuous array of food.

"This is Diana," Cynthia says, as we all sit down. I note a marked resemblance between the two, though Diana looks older by a couple of years. From her voice she too sounds Canadian. She's no caterer! Martin's clearly got this all wrong!

"How nice it is," I say, "that two sisters can share a home together. It used to be quite common until the 1960s. I had two maiden aunts who lived happily together in Tooting Bec until…"

It is the silence that stops me. Harry and Mike are smirking madly, and Martin is tittering quietly to himself, but it is Cynthia's indulgent smile that stops me in my tracks. "Bernie, Diana's not my sister. She's my partner."

"Oh. So you wear a wedding ring just to stop awkward questions?" I responded.

"No. Diana and I are married. We tied the knot in Vancouver in August 2005, just after Canada legalised same-sex marriage."

In the car on the way home, Harry ribs me remorselessly about my blundering naïveté, alternating with smutty speculation about what Cynthia and Diana get up to. Personally, I just want the ground to swallow me up.

Thursday 14ᵗʰ June: Inter Link In The Sink

Read that the bid for Inter Link Foods has collapsed, and Harry's shares will be worth nought. As usual my call comes as a shock to him. Why does he never check news on his investments?

Chapter Sixteen

Kwik Not Saved

Saturday 16th June: Death By Chocolate

Dropped Eunice off at Reflections in the High Street, where she had a long-standing appointment to get miscellaneous body parts (armpits, chin and possibly knuckles) waxed. Told her I thought she'd go rather well in Madame Tussauds, and earned myself a wintry smile. Sensibly, I omitted to mention that I envisaged her propped up in the modern horror section somewhere between Slobodan Milosevic and Gwyneth Dunwoody. Still, while my wife was going through a medieval torture routine (at futuristic prices), I was able to sneak off in search of comestibles. However, arrived at Kwik Save to see the place locked up and empty. Shock! I knew they were forced to close some stores, but surely not this one. The proportion of my MoD pension spent here on KitKats, Bounty bars and Mini Rolls would surely have been enough to keep the place afloat. Moreover, a tattooed granny who worked on the basket-only counter had always promised never to 'grass me up' as she put it, if Eunice came in asking about my purchasing habits.

As I walked along, past a Help the Aged, an Oxfam and a Clintons card shop, I reflected on just how many shops seem to have closed since the giant Tesco opened last year by the motorway. All that is left is the Oddbins, a couple of estate agents, the NatWest bank and the magnificently misnamed Perfick (sic) Pizza, where you pay £5.99 to a deranged Geordie for what appears to be a dandruff-covered cowpat. For an extra £1 they can get a myopic illiterate on a moped to deliver it to a random house in the neighbourhood. Still, it is actually worth the extra pound to ensure someone else gets it. Domino's Pizza, competing in a market like this, has absolutely nothing to worry about. No wonder it's one of my best-performing shares.

Finally found a pound shop and struck gold by the till when I saw a three-for-two deal on Terry's Chocolate Oranges. However, as

155

I smuggled them into the house I noticed they were two months past the best before date. Can chocolate go off? Until the Cadbury salmonella scare I didn't think so. Still, if the idea of death by cholesterol won't put me off, I should be able to manage a week of intestinal agony.

Sunday 17ᵗʰ June: The Cocoa Pusher

Chaotic family tea with my mother, Brian, Janet and, of course Digby, the pre-adolescent Antichrist. Eunice, far from being the attentive hostess, finds half an hour to drone on to Irmgard on the phone, while her long-suffering family wait patiently for food. I take a brief visit to the model railway in the loft, for a moment of blessed peace. A rattling on the stairs indicates the arrival of Digby, who clambers into the loft with an oddly excited expression on his face.

"Guess what I've got, Grandpa," he smirks.

"Not nits I hope," I respond, edging away.

"Look," he whispers, moving closer and offering me a slightly melted chocolate finger.

"Um, not at the moment," I say.

"I thought you liked them," he said. "I've got a whole packet."

"Well, good for you. Does your mother know?"

"'Course not," he sniggered. "She's not into bickies like you and me."

"It's you and I, Digby, " I say as I relieve him of the chocolate and break it into two, one part for each of us. "Not you and me."

Monday 18th June: Ethics Man

I just cannot believe that Lord Woolf is going to get paid £6,000 a day of shareholders' money to paper over the gaping ethical cracks in BAe's business practices (maybe he'll use some of the spare £300 per roll stuff that Lord Irvine used for his office). Everyone knows how it works in the defence industry. You pay lip service to all the codes of practice in the EU and the U.S., tick all the boxes, but do whatever it takes to get the business before the French do. The best advice about bribery in such circumstances is simply "don't get caught", and I offer it for free.

The ridiculous thing is that I find myself defending BAe even though it is my mother, oblivious to everything but the cost of support stockings and the state of her digestive system, who has me in an ever-tight bind of anxiety through her refusal to countenance spreading her portfolio.

Elevenses: A precious segment of Terry's Chocolate Orange. Since my last dual with Eunice over sweets, in which I was disarmed with the Electrolux, I have instituted stealth technology. Instead of using the Hornby drawer, I have cunningly concealed three of these delicious chocolate spheres inside old tennis balls, after having made an incision two-thirds of the way round. The balls are in a shoe box on the floor, now guarded by Prescott, the suede pig.

Tuesday 19th June: Ssschhh, You Know What

Just reading about the shock news of 7,000 job cuts at Cadbury Schweppes. Don't have shares in the firm, though I have to admit I was once tempted, but it now seems the drinks side is to be sold or demerged after some shareholder kerfuffle. Perhaps I'm simplistic, but the idea is mad. Cadbury seems like a portfolio company, balancing cold weather sales of chocolate against heat-induced sales of fizzy drinks. Now it will be at the mercy of the weather, a bit like Thorntons. How is that going to help?

Also noticed the gradual slide in Bovis shares has resumed. Perhaps I should have sold when they were at £12, but I just didn't believe we were going to get a house price slump. Now, however, interest rate rise gloom is getting worse and they are heading back to £9, eroding much of this year's gain. Notice that though the FTSE 100 is holding up alright, the mid-caps are in broad retreat. Looks like Perfect Peter might have been right again to sell in May.

Close of play: My demented mother phones up, complaining that she is being harassed by BT. And it's not for the first time. Last time she imagined she was being followed by a bearded engineer called Tim. This time she claims they are bombarding her with the engaged tone. I have absolutely no idea what she is on about.

"Well, don't leave the phone off the hook," I say, recalling that they do use a loud tone to get you to replace the receiver.

"I didn't. It's coming through the window."

"Mum, don't be ridiculous."

"They've got a van outside. It must be them."

I don't know whether to laugh or cry at the mental deterioration that now seems almost too apparent. "What kind of noise is it? Can you hear it now?" I ask.

"I'm opening the window for a minute, but I don't want to let them in," Dot says. "Can you hear it?"

Good grief. Yes, I actually can clearly hear a beep, beep, beep, beep, with a brief interruption before its resumption. How odd. Hang on a minute. It's the reversing signal for a lorry, surely. I tell Dot this, but she's adamant.

"But the BT van's parked. The man's sitting on the wall eating a kebab."

"What about other lorries, forklift trucks in the warehouse opposite, that kind of thing?" I say, with growing exasperation.

"It can't be them. Why would they use the BT engaged tone?" Dot responds.

"No, Mum. It's not a BT signal. It's what all commercial vehicles use to tell people they are reversing."

"I've never heard it before. Except on the phone."

"Yes you have. It's a health and safety thing, to stop people like you getting run over."

"But uncle Len used to have a milk float, after he got rid of the horse, and that was as quiet as a cat," Dot says.

This is clearly hopeless. After pacifying her as best I can, I replace the receiver, throw open the windows and breath in the fresh garden air. Above the birdsong, far in the distance, I too can hear the sound of the south-east economy. Beep, beep, beep...

Wednesday 20th June: Flushed With Success

Fairly subdued share club meeting. I'm avoiding Cynthia after embarrassing myself last time. Chantelle is hard at work behind the bar, while K.P. Sharma is leafing through *Company Refs* and muttering to himself about PEG ratios (whatever they are). Only Harry Staines and Martin Gale are in high spirits. The reason, it appears, is that they are off to Glastonbury tomorrow. Not for the music. Not even for the wild young women, though I'm sure Harry's bullet-proof self-confidence won't stop him trying. No, they have laid their hands on an old horsebox lorry, which they have kitted out as a green loo. There are five cubicles, charged at 50p a time, wired up to a sound system.

"We've got the greatest hits of Dave Dee, Dozy, Beaky, Mick and Titch, the Rubettes' Christmas Album, and of course, Mud," says Martin, leafing through the K-Tel CDs he got at a boot sale.

"Well, that should be irresistible," I mutter.

"We even got some old David Cameron election leaflets to use as bog roll," enthuses Harry. "Those bra-less leftie birds will love that. We'll make a fortune."

"What about waste disposal? That's pretty expensive," I say.

"No trouble," chuckles Harry. "The toilets run straight out onto the ground. At the end of the festival we just drive away and leave it to rot down. That's why it's green."

"You can't do that, it's illegal! Not to say insanitary."

"They won't notice with all the mud," he says. "Besides, if they dig through to see who dumped it, the only address left behind will be Conservative Party HQ at Millbank."

Thursday 21st June: Eire Of Suspicion

Experienced a Eunice incursion across the border of Lemon Curdistan this morning. Fortunately, I was merely reading a copy of Domino's Pizza's annual report, and checking some share prices.

"Irmgard has just said that we can borrow their holiday cottage in Ireland," she announces, breathlessly.

Her timing was slightly off. I'd just finished a plain chocolate Bounty. I hurriedly stuff the wrapper, which was still in my hand, into the directors' fees section of the report. Eunice, however, is clearly not in gestapo mode today.

"Oh yes?" I say, noncommittally. "It's probably some kind of rusting cowshed with a peat bog back and front and electricity only every other Wednesday."

"Actually, Bernard, it's a purpose-built, three bedroom house with a slate roof, and a fully equipped kitchen with dishwasher, washing machine and tumble dryer, plus views of the sea."

"And how much are we to be charged for this dubious Gaelic privilege?" I inquire.

"For your information, she is letting us have it at half price. Bernard, why do you have to be such an utter misery? You just don't believe my best friend would do anything for us, do you?" she cried.

"Well, she usually has some kind of agenda. It will either have a bloody great windmill on the roof, be part of a manure-sodden organic farm, or coincide with the all-Ireland tinkers reunion just up the road."

"Bernard, I have to hand it to you. You don't just look a gift horse in the mouth. You X-ray the entire beast."

"Don't forget the blood and urine samples," I add.

"Look, do you or don't you want to have a lovely, week-long, half price holiday in Ireland with me? If you don't I shall go alone. Better still, I'll find someone who will. Perhaps I shall get myself a toyboy."

"That's a good idea," I say. "I believe they have some good ones in ToyBoys 'R' Us. I saw an advert for one earlier, just £149.99. Guaranteed for 12 months, comes in kit form but easy to erect with tool kit supplied. Made in China. Heavy duty models will withstand up to 40 stone, so you'll be all right as long as you keep off the Guinness."

"Well it would certainly have some advantages," Eunice

retorted. "You're no great shakes in the erection department, with or without tools." At that, Eunice exited. From the decibel level of the door slam, I reckon that will be a 35-45 minute huff.

Chapter Seventeen

Party Pooper

Saturday 23rd June: Woodwind Party

What joy. Eunice and I have been invited to Irmgard and Nils's home for a party. Billed as an evening of 'light snacks and musical entertainment', we were requested to bring a musical instrument and a whole food dish rather than the normal bottle of wine. Eunice, who claims to be able to sing, has brought no instrument but has rustled up a soy milk, chive and artichoke dip to impress her vegan friend. It actually looks like a bowl of mouldy wallpaper paste, and I shall steer well clear. I have brought along Jem's old school recorder, which I cannot play, and unknown to Eunice, the whoopee cushion that my colleagues at the MoD gave me on my leaving day. Of course, with all the lentils and beans likely to be consumed, I'm pretty sure I will form just a small part of the wind section.

When we arrive, the party is in full swing, but perhaps the type that our former hangman Albert Pierrepoint might have recognised. There are lots of people sporting facial hair, some of them male. There are quite a few droopy-breasted earth mothers in shapeless kaftans sporting necklaces of cowrie shells the size of hubcaps. Someone is plucking at a mandolin of all things, and a cross-eyed waif of no more than seventeen is singing, in a thin and hesitant voice, what she announced as a madrigal. There seem to be an awful lot of odd-smelling hand-rolled cigarettes, and rather a lot of bloodshot eyes.

Nils apologises that they have no gin for my G&T, but suggests that I try the effervescent elderflower champagne. Eunice has a giant glass of nettle wine, which looks exactly like one of the samples I demanded from our gift horse.

Irmgard immediately collars me, and suggests I should sell all my shares to invest in bio-diesel production and cellulose-eating kelp to help global warming. Seeing as we are about to occupy her

Irish holiday home, I listen politely as she talks with the earnestness that only the comfortable middle classes can manage, about the need for utter revolution. This would entail a green jihad in which private equity managers, hedge fund owners and anyone who earns an annual bonus would be forced to undertake agricultural community service with an emphasis on silage and slurry. Only after an hour, when my fixed grin is beginning to ache, do I manage to make my escape, pleading an urgent need for the loo. Eunice meanwhile, is deep in conversation with a Worzel Gummidge look-alike whose shoes are laced with baler twine. He is apparently telling her that British soil is so exhausted by intensive agriculture that we no longer get anything like the amount of essential minerals we used to from our vegetables.

Macheting my way across the living room, through a party of cross-legged tambourine jinglers I contemplate the staircase, jammed with aged but unreconstructed hippies, smoking, necking and groping as if they were sixteen. Finding a foothold, I begin my solo ascent, without oxygen. Once I get in to the most sought-after room, I find that there is an incumbent. A comatose young man, fully dressed and with a toy trumpet, is giggling to himself in the bath (which has no water in it.) I ask him to leave, but he says though he would like to, he cannot.

"Have a toke of my spliff if you like," he says, waving a soggy-looking cigarette towards me. "It's Leb gold, straight from the Bekaa Valley. You'll be out of your brain in no time."

"I prefer to remain within my brain, thank you all the same. Are you aware that cannabis makes you schizophrenic?" I say.

He finds this hysterically funny. "No wonder I'm beside myself," he finally says.

When I eventually go downstairs, I find Eunice squashed on a crowded sofa with three unkempt young males, earnestly discussing what they all agree is the absurdity of drug laws. One, who cannot be older than twenty-five, has an arm around her shoulder, and his hand, complete with charity wristbands and dirty fingernails is dangling perilously close to her cleavage, like a bungee jumper contemplating some gigantic wrinkled chasm. She looks blearily up at me and I realise she is drunk, or worse. She turns to her companion and says something, and he passes her his joint. Keeping her eyes fixed on me she inhales deeply, daring me to say something. She then exhales a cloud of controlled substance fumes towards me.

"Bernard, this is Paul. Paul, this...superannuated vision in corduroy trousers, carefully polished shoes and blue blazer is my husband. We've been married since before the Boer War."

"Hi man, how y'doin?" Paul asks.

"I'm well, thank you. Eunice, I think perhaps we should go. Time's getting on."

"Yeah, it's nearly 10.30," Paul giggles. "That's pretty late."

"Paul is a very special and sensitive man, Bernard. You could learn a lot from him. He's interested in what a woman has to say. He listens. He's attentive. Unlike you, he can admit to emotions."

"Really? I'm sure that pity is currently the strongest of them," I say as I extend an arm to help Eunice to her feet. She however, leans away from me and plants a wet and lingering kiss on the youth's astonished mouth. "I'm going to Ireland next month," she croons to her perplexed paramour. "If my husband doesn't want to go, you can be my toyboy."

Paul, whose sangfroid has been severely disturbed by having his face Dysoned, is now impersonating a terrified bushbaby.

"Er. That's really kind. But my girlfriend has invited me to the South of France."

Finally, as I lever an unsteady Eunice to her feet and steer her out of the room, I turn to Paul and mutter. "I do hope she didn't ask for your phone number?"

"Er..." he said.

"You didn't tell her, did you?"

"Er..."

"For pity's sake, man. Don't you have any instinct for self-preservation? She'll badger you to death. You may have to move house. The last one had to get a court order to keep her away." A lie perhaps, but better than creating the jealous scene that Eunice so earnestly wanted.

Chapter Eighteen

Password Bingo

Monday 25th June: Ming The Merciless

6pm. Northern England has been walloped with a month's rain in a day, and there are moving accounts of people's homes being ruined by floodwaters. Eunice's appalling sister Veronica, who lives on the outskirts of Leeds, phones up for the first time since Christmas to say that she and Douglas have had all their Axminsters ruined, the koi carp (£68 each) have been flopping about on the geranium bed, and described how the Canadian maple decking (£1,438 plus VAT) is now bound to start splitting. How awful. After wringing out my dishcloth of sympathy I pass the phone to Eunice, willing her with all my mind not to say what I just *know* she is going to say, and which is exactly what Veronica wants her to say.

"Well, Veronica this is a very sorry tale indeed," Eunice said. "Why don't you and Douglas come to stay with us for a few days? Just until you get yourselves sorted out."

Eunice puts the phone down and wags a finger at me even before I've had a chance to voice my objections.

"Bernard, I know what you are going to say. And yes, she is a pain. But how can I refuse? She is my sister after all."

Indeed. Eunice was only a practice run in the DNA of insufferability. Veronica is a full-on motor mouth, the woman who put the gob in Goebbels. She'll ask the price of everything and pay for nothing. And Douglas will drone on and on about his newly restored MGB even though he knows it bores everyone witless.

Then the final rancid cherry on the gateau. Ming, their vile, boss-eyed psychotic pekingese is coming too. This dog bites every hand that feeds it, has a piercing yip, and true to its name, smells perpetually of vomit. They arrive on Friday. What joy!

Tuesday 26th June: Revenge Of The Feds

Forget rainfall – the disaster I had really feared has happened. The U.S. Department of Justice is investigating BAe Systems. Criminal prosecution of managers, unlimited fines, independent oversight and potentially being excluded from its main source of business. Oh, the pain of being able to foresee this and do nothing about it! The shares are down almost 10%. That's £60,000 of the Jones family's potential inheritance down the drain, and all because my lunatic mother refuses to let me balance her portfolio. I actually jump up and down in frustration.

"What on earth's the matter, Bernard?" Eunice says as she bursts into the den with flour on her hands.

"Look at this," I say pointing at the *Telegraph* web site on the screen. "I knew this would happen."

"Well it's her money to use as she pleases," Eunice says. "I don't know why you make such a fuss. Stop jumping about or you'll give yourself an embolism."

3.45pm. Astounding discovery! Was digging on the floor through a pile of old *Chronic Investor* magazines, when I find the first statement on Dot's brokerage account from last year. Scribbled on the top is my mother's e-mail address and password. I had it in the den all the time! Logging in, I find that she has been deluged with the usual junk, and nothing has been cleared for months. I know she changed the password on the broker's website with Clive's help, so I click the 'forgotten password' button and was told that a reminder would be sent. Is it too late? I have no idea.

In all this fuss, forgot that Gordon Brown is now being inflicted on us as PM. Heard a great new Labour Party motto idea on Radio 4: Things can only get wetter.

Wednesday 27th June: An Astounding Discovery

Password reminder arrives in Dot's e-mail account from her broker. Guess what it is? THIEFBERNARD. What an outrage! All I'm trying to do is stop her losing her money, the daft old bat. BAe is down again to 410p, compared to 470p in February. Log in to Dot's account. Shock! Not a single BAe Systems share in there. Panic briefly, and double check the name and account number. Yes, definitely correct. It is Dot's account. What it does contain are holdings in Laura Ashley, Dignity the funeral directors, Mothercare, Marks & Spencer, British Airways, Smith & Nephew, Bloomsbury Publishing, Carnival the cruise line, and Care UK, oh and a great wodge of gilts. Total value £690,000. My God, she's even made some money. I print out the last three months' transactions and find they were all made on one day, Monday 5th February. She must have had some help. It's a portfolio for sure, and a bit heavy on retailers and healthcare, but it's far better than what she had before. I just cannot believe this piece of extraordinary luck! I really want to find out who helped her. Trouble is, if she discovers that I've been snooping into her account she'll probably cut me out of her will altogether.

Chapter Nineteen

Racquet And Reckitt

Thursday 28th June: Portfolio Jam

Take a trip round to my mother's to try to discover more about who reorganised her portfolio. Dot is watching Wimbledon on TV, though of course that means watching repeats of last year because of the rain. "I haven't seen Ken Rosewall," she says.

"He retired decades ago, Mum."

"Who's that then?"

"That's called an umpire. He's a kind of referee. Notice the absence of whites, a racquet or balls."

"Oh. And when's Nastase on?"

"He's stopped too, years ago," I say. "You can watch Roger Federer thrash some Croat called Gamesoonova or something at 4pm. How about that?"

"Never heard of either of them. I'll wait for Andy Henman."

While Dot witters on, I ask her whether she has made any new friends recently, such as stockbrokers or financial advisers.

"I wouldn't trust a stockbroker," Dot says. "They're just after your money. No, if I want some common sense I go to the WI."

"The Women's Institute!" I squeal. "Running a share portfolio isn't like making jam you know. The stock market will eat them for breakfast. On toast, I expect."

However, I have to admit that I can't put much passion into the complaint having seen the rather reasonably balanced portfolio that Dot now has. If that's the work of the WI, perhaps I'll go along to the next meeting myself.

Friday 29th June: Law Of Relativity

Veronica and Douglas arrived at noon. Ming, the vile pekingese, was already scratching at the front door and yipping before Veronica had even pressed the doorbell. The wheezing, flat-faced creature had already found time to leave a steaming deposit on the lawn, which both guests studiously ignored, and no sooner was it inside the house it got so excited it vomited. While Eunice wielded the kitchen roll and carpet shampoo, I got the full Veronica verbal steamroller, beginning with an exhaustive list of everything damaged by the flood, and of course its value. To listen to my sister in-law you'd think that she lived in the Taj Mahal rather than a dreary semi on the outskirts of Leeds. Douglas whispered that after two hours of hectoring, the insurer's loss adjustor had barricaded himself in his Mondeo to get away from her.

Took Douglas up into the loft to show him the railway layout, but he merely picked holes in the historical consistency of the motor vehicles I had queuing at the level crossing. A wheezing and scratching noise heralded the arrival of Ming, who somehow had scaled the loft ladder. Most alarmingly, it had a tennis ball in its mouth, presumably one of those in which I had concealed a Terry's Chocolate Orange. Worse still, it was attempting to chew it. As I desperately attempted to swipe the ball, the microscopic mutt turned tail and scampered down the ladder, and I chased him into our bedroom. Douglas couldn't understand my urgency in pursuing the dog, but Ming thought it was great fun.

"Come on Ming, nice doggie. Give it here, there's a good little rodent," I said as I approached, left hand out towards it, rolled up *Railway Modeller* concealed in the other. Ming then jumped on the bed, leaving a trail of melted chocolate across our Egyptian cotton counterpane. With no time to lose I let fly, whacking the verminous fluff-ball across the head. Unfortunately, Veronica had chosen just this moment to emerge from the bathroom. Her shrieks and the pitiful whimpering of the dog merged into one, and once Eunice arrived I got it in the neck on charges of chocolate concealment too. Much tutting and recrimination over grievous doggily harm. My punishment was to drive to the shops to get some super-charged cleaning products for carpets and bedclothes.

"Douglas," Eunice said. "Would you go with him? Make sure he doesn't buy anything edible. If it doesn't have Reckitt Benckiser or Procter & Gamble written on the side, he can't have it."

Sunday 1ˢᵗ July: Cheap ~~Housebuilders~~

Catching up on share research, I notice that housebuilder Bovis, having been worth £12.25 in April, has stabilised at £9. This had made a big hole in my gains, which had exceeded the FTSE but no longer do. It's still pretty cheap in P/E terms, so decide I should buy more ahead of the trading statement next week.

Monday 2ⁿᵈ July: Big Mac And Biodiesel

McDonalds says it is to run its entire fleet of 155 UK delivery vehicles on surplus chip fat to save 1,650 tonnes of carbon a year. A nice little PR stunt no doubt, but all this jumping on the green bandwagon seems a little suspicious to me. For the company that appeased its critics by offering more salads, and then deluged the greenery with dressings that make a Big Mac look like a slice of Slimcea, this is probably just another ruse. It might have been better to get the vans to run on the burger component that everyone throws away: gherkins.

 Elevenses: A broken macaroon of pensionable age which I found under the signal box on my layout. Presumably secreted there during some ancient cholesterol siege. Following the chocolate orange debacle, I must show the greatest circumspection with Eunice. With the local Kwik Save now closed, I have to get the car out to get a decent range of cakes or biscuits, and that always alerts the trouble and strife.

Thursday 5th July: Chronic Veronica

Douglas, Veronica and their evil canine homunculus are departing today, off to inflict themselves on poor Felicity in Herne Bay. Thank the Lord. After a week of Douglas's conversation, I could easily pen a non-best seller: *Everything you always wanted to know about MGB carburettors (but were afraid to ask)*. Veronica claims to have suffered two migraine attacks, an ongoing dose of irritable bowel syndrome, plus ulcerative colitis, the full details of which we have not been spared. The queue for getting into a bathroom here over the last week makes securing a seat for a Wimbledon singles final seem a doddle. Veronica has even infuriated Eunice by complaining about her food. ("Sorry, dear, but fennel and aubergine go straight through me without slowing down for corners. What about a nice bit of rump steak?") Now, on the final day, Veronica has developed a hacking cough, which she puts down to the damp, but which I think is really bovine TB. Perhaps we should do to her what Defra does to infected badgers.

Chapter Twenty

Emerald Isle Trial

Friday 6th July: Dis-united Ireland

Eunice and I are off to Ireland, without toyboy but instead with family baggage: Brian, Janet and the mischievous tyke Digby. The recalcitrant child had to be told three times by the stewardess to stop playing with his PlayStation during take-off, and then sulked when I took the thing off him. I'm not sure whether it really does interfere with the plane's electronics as they claim, but it certainly interferes with mine. We've been together just five hours and already the beep-beep-beep in the car on the M25, in the Gatwick check-in queue and then the departure lounge is driving me to distraction.

Security restrictions do seem to be getting worse. Took four trips through the electronic door, finally without shoes or watch, before the machine would agree that I wasn't a member of Al-Aqsa Martyrs' Brigade (Beckenham and Orpington Branch). Eunice caused a similar security frisson behind me, which turned out to be not a suicide vest but brassiere underwiring, an overly hefty zip and suspender belt buckles. It's like travelling with a cross between Robocop and Zsa Zsa Gabor.

Arrived at Shannon Airport and, naturally enough, it is pouring. Hire car place has a long queue, and then it's a long wait for the courtesy bus, then the car's not ready (they've not cleaned the vomit out of the passenger footwell yet) so we get upgraded to a people carrier. This pleases everyone except me, because the damn thing appears to be wider than most Irish lanes. I've got the minimum level of collision damage waiver insurance, and the excess is €2,000. As the rain hammers down I get the clerk to note every microscopic ding, dent and hairline crack.

"Oh, come on Bernard. We're getting soaked," Eunice says, while I crouch to examine the sills and wheel archs.

"Look. You know what these people are like. Every scratch has to be noted or you pay for it. Some dents have paid for themselves 50 times over, I'm sure." That earned me a very sour look from the clerk.

Finally we were off, and straight into an enormous traffic jam. Eunice, doing the map-reading, plunges us into a Friday night rush hour. "I can't seem to avoid this place Luimneach," she says, it's on all the signposts, but it's not on my map."

"Let's have a look," Brian says, reaching forward to grab at the vast cartographical piece of guesswork Eunice is now fully unfolding.

"Not in front of me," I say. "I can't see the bloody road if you do that! I can hardly see through the spray anyway."

"Well stop a minute and let's see where we are," Eunice retorts.

"How can I stop? I'm in the right hand filter that you directed me to. We'll be across in four changes or so. Where should we be heading?"

"We're supposed to be heading north-west to Doolin, away from Limerick," she said. "Doolin's up here," she says, flashing a large part of the map in front of me again.

"But isn't this Limerick?" I reply. "I'm sure I saw it on a sign."

"No, this is Luimneach, I told you."

"Well, it's pretty damn big, it should be on the map."

"Perhaps Luimneach is Limerick, but in Gaelic?" Brian suggests.

"I hope not, because that means we heading exactly the wrong way," I say, adding: "Digby, for Christ's sake will you stop beeping away on that machine!"

"No need to yell," says Janet. "At least it's keeping him occupied."

"Yes, like the Germans kept Poland occupied," I snarled.

"Bernard, do calm down," Eunice said.

"Look," says Brian. "That signs says city centre for both Limerick and Luimneach. So it was just in Gaelic."

"Oh, they're just the same as the bloody Welsh," I sigh. "The moment you cross the border the signs become incomprehensible and unpronounceable. It's all a ruse to annoy the English."

"It's certainly working then," Eunice notes tartly.

This witless badinage continues for the hour it takes us to navigate to the centre of town, where we are hemmed in by roadworks while a giant crane is manoeuvred into a building site.

"I was expecting country lanes and horse-drawn carts," said Janet wistfully, staring at the four-wheel-drive gridlock ahead of us.

"That's a vibrant economy for you," says Brian. "Ireland's been booming for years, ever since they sensibly joined the euro. But of course we Brits wouldn't do it, would we?"

My schoolteacher son never wastes an opportunity to cross political swords with me, whether it is hectoring me about the evil of shares or why Britain has never been an enthusiast for Europe.

"Still, Brian, it is housebuilding that's driving the Irish economy. See how new many of these homes are? You might remember that when you have a go at me for my shareholding in Bovis, or whinge about the Barratt boxes over the back. Housebuilding is a great economic force."

An hour later we navigate our way north out of Limerick, on a country lane heading for Ennis.

"What's the Gaelic for Ennis, Eunice? Just in case we get another of those signs," I say.

"Don't ask me. I don't speak the lingo."

We then see, through the still-torrential rain, a sign which says 'Inis 5km' and below has a spray painted line through the English translation, and then one word of greeting: 'Provos.'

"Typical," I say. "Just typical. They still hate us, after all we've done for them."

"Stop being such a xenophobe, Bernard," Eunice says, as she directs me left. "This is a short cut," she adds. Five miles later we reach a crossroads where there are no signs at all.

"Which way now?" I ask.

"Search me," says Eunice. "Probably right," she says turning the map upside down with a great crackling and flapping noise.

"What are you doing that for?" I ask.

"If I put the map in the direction we're travelling it's easier to follow," she insists. "Turn left."

"You said it was right a minute ago."

"No, left. Sorry, straight on."

By the time we finally reach Doolin it is 9.45pm. We find the house, a few kilometres outside the town, with characteristic difficulty, but just as we do so the rain stops.

"It's really lovely," says Janet.

She's right. It's a pretty house with a well-kept garden, and is immaculate. Barely a trace of hippy activity, no leftie posters, no vegan leftovers, water bongs, or 'exotic' houseplants and even the windows are clean. It's hard to believe that Irmgard and Nils have owned this place for long.

Saturday 7th July: Heir Apparent

A fine morning. Up early and take a brisk walk with Digby down to the cliffs. Sea birds are soaring over the sparkling sea and the roar of foam against rocks is uplifting. For a moment I feel elated, and then as I turn round to my irksome grandson I hear it:

Beep-beep-beep.

"Digby, for goodness sake, put that thing away. Look! This is nature's beauty. There's more to life than a silly screen."

"But Grandad! I've only got two zombies left to zap and I get up to twelfth level," he replied.

"Look. We've got three zombies still sleeping it off back at the house. Zap them with a cup of tea when we get back and I'm sure they'll give you a medal."

Reluctantly, Digby pockets his toy and gazes out. "Which sea is this?"

"It's the Atlantic Ocean. Next stop New York! Isn't that exciting?"

"Are there great whites sharks in it?"

"Not here, I shouldn't think. There might be dolphins though."

"Cool."

"So, have you given any thought to what you'd like to be when you grow up?"

He thought for a moment then said: "I want to be Spiderman."

"Hmm. You can't actually *be* Spiderman because he doesn't exist. But perhaps a web designer?"

A small smile showed he got the joke. "Grandad, when Great-

Grandma dies, will I get some of her money?"

"Digby, that's really not a nice thought to have. It's really rare to know a great-grandmother. You should treasure her while she's still alive, and forget about money."

"But...."

"What, Digby?"

"But Grandma says it's you who won't stop talking about her money," Digby said.

That shuts me up completely. I suddenly feel a wave of guilt.

Sunday 8ᵗʰ July: Monopoly Commissioned

Raining again. Third game of Monopoly dominated, once again, by our devious little private equity fiend. After winning the first two games, Digby again managed to amass all the stations, Regent Street, Bond Street and Oxford Street, plus Mayfair and Park Lane with hotels. My only possessions, Pall Mall and the water and electricity utilities, paid me few dividends because Digby never landed on them, and I only caught poor Janet and Brian who had already been taken to the cleaners. Eunice made the mistake of buying everything she could lay hands on and then mortgaging it, but had retained four houses each from Strand to Trafalgar Square. Digby, kneeling on his chair and almost drooling with megalomania grabbed the dice for his turn, and from Vine Street rolled a three and a one.

"Aha," Eunice squawked. "Street of Shame. That's mine! £875 please, Digby."

"No, that was a five and one," Digby bellowed, grabbing the dice. "Fenchurch Street! Mine!"

"Digby, that's wrong," Janet said gently.

"Come on Onassis, cough up!" I chuckled.

"No! It's NOT FAIR."

"What do you mean, 'not fair' you've got piles of cash!" I said.

Suddenly Digby swiped his arm across the board and sent everything tumbling to the ground. "Not FAIR," he yelled and ran upstairs.

There was an embarrassed silence before Brian said. "Right. That's it." He thundered upstairs and I thought, fantastic, he's really going to give the child the thrashing that he so richly deserves. But no. After the bedroom door closed I waited in vain. No swish of the cane, no crack of the belt, no fizz of an electric chair. Not even the smack of a hand. I walked upstairs and listened at the door.

"That wasn't right Digby."

"Go away. I hate you." Beep-beep-beep.

"No you don't."

"Do too." Beep-beep-beep.

"You mustn't inflict your anger on others."

Beep-beep-beep.

"Digby…"

Beep-beep-beep-beep.

The door opened, and Brian walked out.

"That told him then, didn't it?" I said.

Brian's look of resignation said it all.

Monday 9ᵗʰ July: Say It With Flowers

Finally the rain stopped. Took a long and congested afternoon drive along the coast. Get tired of trundling along at 15mph and seeing nothing but the back of the camper van in front, and its irritating sticker 'naughty person on board'. For our car we'd have to have 'wicked little psychopath on board'.

Pulled over to see the cliffs and to walk on the Burren's limestone pavement. We're just a few yards from the car, but Eunice pulls from her handbag a large hardback: *A Field Guide to Orchids*.

"Now then, what have we here?" she says pointing to a tiny, wilted purple flower.

"It's a tiny wilted purple flower," I say.

"Ah, but is it a tiny wilted southern marsh orchid, or tiny wilted pyramidal orchid?"

Janet joins in stooping over the thing. Digby comes round to have a look and by mistake treads on it.

"Digby!" says Eunice. "You've squashed it, poor thing."

"What?" he says. "What?"

"The flower!" Eunice says. As he steps back, we survey the wreckage. Twisted stem, and only one petal left. Digby runs off, while Eunice and Janet tut away. A few yards away they find something else worthy of note.

"Ooh look, bloody cranesbill," she says.

"Yes, its all over the bloody place. Look, there's a whole bloody field of it over there," I say.

"Bernard, its name is bloody cranesbill. Stop trying to be clever."

I wander off to look at the cliffs and find a rock to perch on from which I can feel the swell of the sea, and the roar of the surf. Then I hear some beeping, and turn round to see my grievous grandson approaching, PlayStation akimbo.

"For goodness sake, Digby. Give it to me," I say, prising the wretched machine from his grasp. "Look at all this beauty!" I say, waxing lyrical as I point out the spray-wreathed headland. "Fill your soul with flowers, sea and cliffs! Use *your* imagination, not that of some spotty programmer at Sony. This is nature's playground, use it!"

Digby pouts and shuffles off, clearly bored. A few minutes later I see him crouching down in the distance, perhaps tracking some beetle as it makes away across the rocks, or looking for quartz crystals. As he looks up at me, I nod approvingly. He's got something in his hands as he heads off towards Eunice, Brian and Janet. Perhaps he's found an interesting geological specimen. I'm sure with his intelligence Digby could become a normal healthy boy, if he would just give up the silly computer games.

As he rejoins the group I watch the reaction, and it isn't quite as I expected. Whatever it is that he gives Eunice instantly enrages here. Some stern finger wagging follows, and Digby responds then by pointing towards me. Eunice for some reason looks daggers in my direction, and I have a familiar but no less terrifying feeling that I'm in trouble. My wife, wearing the determination of a First World War subaltern crossing no-man's land, marches purposefully towards me.

"Bernard, what on earth have you been telling him!"

"Nothing, why?"

"Did you tell him to give me a bunch of flowers?"

"Of course not."

"He says you took his PlayStation away. Did you?"

"Yes, I wanted him to enjoy nature instead."

"Well, I tell you what he's done. He's picked a huge bunch of pyramidal and southern marsh orchids, plus heaven forbid, a bee orchid of all rarities. He said they were for me, from you."

"They were nothing to do with…"

"Bernard, do you have the *first idea* how rare and endangered they are? These are protected species! Next thing you'll be taking him to Borneo with an air rifle on an orangutan shooting safari."

"Don't be ridiculous," I said.

"I despair of you Bernard, really I do. If we get caught it's either a whopping great fine or imprisonment."

"Oh. Well, what's the age of criminal responsibility in Ireland?" I asked. "He should be able to get bail."

"Bernard, he's a nine-year-old child. We'll get jailed, not him. It's our responsibility…"

"Brian and Janet's, dear…"

"Neither Brian nor Janet asked him to start digging up rare plants…"

"I didn't bloody suggest it either!" I roared.

"Digby insists that when he started pulling them up, you nodded at him so he carried on."

"I had no idea what he was doing. I though he was looking at insects or rocks. If he'd only use his common sense…"

"Bernard, the child is nine!" Eunice then grabbed at my pocket and dug out the PlayStation. "Don't you realise that it's much less trouble all round when he has this to play with? In future just leave well alone."

Driving back, in the newly lashing rain, all I could hear above the frosty silence in the back seat was beep-beep-beeping, gnawing away at my nerves like relentless mocking laughter. As I glared at the child in the mirror, he looked up at me, and a sly and mischievous grin slid across his face. I think he planned it this way all along.

Tuesday 10ᵗʰ July: Conway's Bar

Eunice and I take an evening off from monster-sitting for Brian and Janet, and go out for some respite for ourselves. Found ourselves in Ballykilldannyone, or some such town. Presumably named after an IRA member's defence plea. However, must say that the locals are disarmingly friendly. Before the meal, Eunice suggested we go into a bar, and there must have been fifty to choose from. In search of authenticity of atmosphere she chose the smallest and dingiest, Conway's. As we walked into the single dusty room, there was a cheery but incomprehensible welcome from the barmaid, and two weather-beaten and cloth-capped locals.

Seeing the Guinness sign and little else, I ordered a pint. Eunice hummed and hawed and then said, in best Tunbridge Wells. "I'd like a Dubonnet with cold lemonade and a slice of fresh lime."

I caught the eye of one of the locals and looked heavenward, in a wordless attempt at male bonding. His jolly face didn't twitch, except for a quick wink at the prospect of my ridiculous wife behaving as if she was in Monte Carlo. I then turned to look at the barmaid, and was surprised to see she was indeed preparing what was asked for.

"Now you didn't think we'd have it, did you mister?" the girl said as she topped up my Guinness. "Thought she'd have to make do with a tot of Paddy's and a lump of ice?"

"Not at all," I lied. "I had every confidence."

"You're full of it, to be sure. That's what you are," she replied cheerfully.

We then got into conversation with the two elderly men, who wanted to know where we came from and what we were doing in Ireland.

"So are you after buying a holiday cottage then?" said the man with the twinkly eyes, whose name was Danny.

"No, we're using one owned by a friend," I replied.

He then described to us the unprecedented boom that was sweeping across Ireland, and the economic growth fuelled by housebuilding. "In my father's day, we used to use a pony and trap to get around. Now, look at my car."

He pointed out of the window to a spanking new BMW X5 sitting outside the bar. "If the English had joined the Eurozone like we did, you'd be driving a car like that."

"Well, I do own a Volvo," I responded.

"Yes Bernard, but it's old," said Eunice. "This gentleman is right. If we'd joined the euro we'd have low interest rates like Ireland, and no unemployment."

"I can't see how signing up to a federal European superstate would have done anything except to add heaps of bureaucracy and put us at the mercy of Brussels," I said.

"Oh, sounds like yon feller here is a candidate for UKIP," said not-Danny.

"Not at all," I replied.

"Now to be sure, lady," said Danny, sliding an arm around Eunice's shoulder. "Don't you thing that yer feller here has a passing resemblance to the Robert Kilroy-Silks of this world?"

"Not in my wildest dreams, I'm afraid. My husband, I am forced to admit, has a face better suited for radio," Eunice said, smirking at her wit.

I sighed and looked at my watch. It was a quarter to eight. "I suppose it's time we should be getting back."

"Bernard, don't be absurd. We only just got here!"

"Well. I think I need a breath of air." I stepped outside and wandered up the street. The lights were still on in an estate agency and I looked into the window. Certainly prices were high, but there was some lovely property there. Inside, a rather shapely woman with an elfin hair-do and nice cheekbones was on the phone, and she swivelled around in her chair to smile at me. A couple of minutes later she hung up and came out to see me.

"Anything caught your eye?" she said, with a puckish grin.

"Oh, I'm not really in the market at the moment, thanks."

"Well, we've got plenty of investment property suitable for the overseas buyer as well as holiday homes and apartments."

I hesitated for a moment, and she cajoled me inside to show me some brochures. Within a couple of minutes her twinkling eyes, charm and humour had elicited my name, address, phone number and e-mail. As she locked up for the evening, I returned to Conway's, weighed down with brochures but with a spring in my step.

"I see you've met the charming Fionnuala Quilty," said not-Danny, nodding at the brochures. "She's a wonder, to be sure. Could sell joke collections to a funeral director."

Danny and not-Danny cackled merrily at each other.

"Yes. She's absolutely delightful," I said, then as I caught Eunice's eye added: "Verbally, I mean."

"She's really called the market right," said not-Danny. "Made herself quite wealthy buying off-plan in Limerick. Of course she's drawn in lots of these overseas investors too. Now there's no stamp duty for the first €127,000."

I gazed in wonder at these two elderly gents, who for all the world looked like impoverished sheep farmers, talking about off-plan investing with the same familiarity as the price of a pint. However, my prejudices were not all in vain.

"And she's got the loveliest firm arse," said Danny, flexing the fingers of both hands appreciatively. Then he leaned over to Eunice and added: "Present company excepted, you understand."

"Yes, it is getting quite late, isn't it?" Eunice said, slipping off the bar stool and wrapping her cardigan around her. "Come on, Bernard, let's go back to the house for a mug of hot chocolate. I'm sure Digby would like you to read him a bedtime story."

Chapter Twenty-One

Safe As Houses

Wednesday 11th July: Bovis Plunge

Get back from holiday to discover that Bovis has nose-dived after its trading statement on Monday. I paid 925p for another 200 shares before I left, and now they're worth just 800p and falling. Sales are static, despite prices being held steady. Hopes for a 10 per cent profit increase have evaporated, as has all the money I ever made on this benighted stock. Perhaps I should sell the lot before interest rates go up another notch. Still, this could be an overreaction. Give them another day or two and they'll almost certainly recover somewhat. Sell into the bounce, that's the idea.

Receive a postcard from Perfect Peter Edgington and family in Vladivostok, having completed the first stage of their monumental trans-Siberian rail journey. Can't begin to decipher his handwriting. Perhaps he is telling me he has taken a day off to negotiate his way into the Sakhalin oil field in place of Shell, or perhaps he has bought some high-yielding Mongolian state bonds. I have no idea. What I do know is that on the proceeds of his investing he could take his entire family on a two-month trip across nine time zones, from the wonders of the Hermitage in Leningrad, the Kremlin, a boat trip on the Volga, and on to the endless steppes and taiga of Siberia. With the proceeds of my investing I could just about take Eunice on a bus trip to the chiropodist.

Thursday 12th July: QinetiQ Bid Rumours

Finmeccanica, an Italian firm, is rumoured to be interested in buying QinetiQ. At 187p, the market is clearly not taking the reports seriously. After all, who would want it? It seems that since flotation, QinetiQ has lost as much MoD work as it has gained elsewhere. I paid 210p, and after a peak of 215p in January it's just been gradually downhill ever since, like a bibulous permanent secretary.

Monday 16th July: City Snickers

On the way back from visiting the old MoD boys in town. Rather a splendid evening with some fine anecdotes, but as usual the journey home takes the edge off the fun. At London Bridge, two drunken City oafs lurch in and plonk themselves opposite. One is a tall ginger fellow in pinstripes with a trace of vomit on his lapels, the other a fat, balding chap wearing tasselled loafers and a self-satisfied smirk. While I divide my attention between reading a moth-eaten copy of *Metro* and staring out at the squalid rain-lashed council estates of south-east London, I am forced to listen to them arguing about whether it is four or six of the money-markets team who've actually rogered Caroline in derivatives, and who collects the winnings from the resulting bets. Then it is the turn of drinking boasts.

"Listen Giles, I'm not half as trolleyed tonight as I was at the Nurses Ball. Fourteen bottles of Krug we got through at our table. Fixed income, stupid farts, could only manage nine."

"That's cods, Barney. We had two bottles of Dow 30-year-old port before we even got started. Besides, with Hinchcliffe footing the bill we knew we'd be able to top up at the Ivy later on." Then it was yachts, cars, and inevitably, how they plan to spend their massive bloody bonuses.

After fifteen minutes of this I had, for a lifelong thoroughbred Tory, a very strange sensation. I could detect the rising sap of what I could only describe as Socialism coursing through my veins. How these braying wastrels could do with a few years hewing coal, or working in a care home wiping elderly bottoms at minimum wage, or boiling their brains in a cavernous BT call centre, repeating the same cheery mantra daily until it feels like brainwashing. Indeed, they would be well employed manufacturing almost anything except the global financial mayhem for which they and their kin are currently responsible. Even the demonic curse (Nationalise!) flickered through my brain in time with the staccato rhythm of lamps as we sped through Hither Green station. As I stared into the darkened window, I caught my reflection, looking for all the world like a dour version of Neil Kinnock. Perish the thought!

But what, actually, was I achieving in this life in which my daily financial attentions are with ever-diminishing crumbs, and these smug people decide our future? As we sped through Orrington station, I thought about Amelia Wrigley. Apparently living here since about 1963. Every day I have thought about her. Every day, wondering what might have been had her family not moved to Australia. If there is something I am learning though, it is that it is never too late. Perhaps this week, I shall do some further research into the whereabouts of my first and greatest love. I looked back at the window and smiled at my reflection. Kinnock, thank God, was gone.

Tuesday 17th July: Raised Eyebrows

Had just finished breakfast when I noticed Eunice staring at me. "Bernard, I really think you should trim your eyebrows. You resemble a cross between Denis Healey and the Surrey Puma."

"I'll get it sorted when I next go to the barber's."

"But look at this one," she said, advancing on me, and seizing one unfortunate bristle in a fierce grip. "I mean, it's like something from the roof of GCHQ. Can you receive BBC World Service on it?" With a sharp tug, she plucked it out.

"Ow. For God's sake, Eunice, I'm having breakfast! If you want to play 'Detention at Abu Ghraib', have the patience to wait until I'm finished."

"Don't exaggerate. I'm just improving your grooming. I don't want people to say I married Catweazle."

Chapter Twenty-Two

Carbon Economising

Wednesday 18th July: Share Club Re-vamp

First share club meeting for a while. The portfolio, two per cent up for the year, trails the FTSE. However, we have some stars. BHP Billiton, which reached £15.50 at one stage, is up thirty-four per cent since purchase. Cynthia's BSkyB pick is up twenty-four per cent, BT is up six per cent, but most of the rest are lower. Oakdene Homes and Debt Free Direct are particularly disappointing, having fallen around twenty per cent. The question is what we do now. The discussion falls into two camps. K.P. Sharma and Chantelle feel the market is about to fall, and we should take profits on winners.

"Look," says Chantelle. "BHP is a bet on continuing tightness in metals, which wouldn't survive a recession. BSkyB is a bet on discretionary spending, so ditto. We should only keep BT, plus the rest that aren't doing so well."

"Selling winners and running losers is a recipe for losing money," Cynthia says. "Even in a recession."

However, K.P. reckons the losers are already bargains and won't fall much further. "We should sell what is over-valued," he says. "If something is already a bargain, why should we sell it?"

"But K.P. you can't equate something that has fallen in value to a bargain," Cynthia insists. "Prices often drop because you can't rely on the profit forecasts the forward P/E is based on."

"Do you think we should hold, Harry?" I say, turning to our oldest member who has been distracted by a new and busty barmaid bending over to wipe the table.

"I'd hold them both," he says, absentmindedly.

Cynthia has a huge, in-built voting majority, given how much of the money is hers, but diplomatically agrees a compromise. We sell Oakdene and Ashtead, which has lost only four per cent, take profits on BSkyB and keep the proceeds in cash.

Martin Gale, silent for most of the discussion has decided to sell his iSoft shares, now that the 58p bid from IBA Health of Australia, launched in May, looked certain. He'd paid 390p for them in January 2006, doubled up a month later when they fell to 180p, courtesy of a £6,000 secured loan. "I'm gutted to lose so much, but what can I do?" he said.

Thursday 19th July: Carbon Footprints

Dragooned into a Waitrose shopping expedition with Eunice. Two hours made dull by the worthiness with which it is undertaken. However, between grabbing organic pine nuts and sheep's milk cheese, Eunice bemoans the rising price of basic foods from which even the sainted John Lewis Partnership cannot protect her. The multi-seed filling-smasher rustic loaf she favours is 5p more expensive than usual, the organic Andean peasant-gathered muesli is up 20p and fruit juices seem to have soared to about 80p a litre from below 50p. To me this inflationary lift seems trifling compared with the financial destruction caused by our Godzilla of a council tax bill. However, for Eunice it typifies the wickedness of globalisation, a coterie of evil biofuel makers stealing food from the starving, and the approach of climatic Armageddon.

"I think you're right, dear," I say. "Perhaps we should sell your Clio and get you a bicycle. That will get rid of the pounds and give you a shapely pair of carbon footprints."

The look I got for this entirely reasonable suggestion must have curdled the entire aisle of Yeo Valley organic milk.

Friday 20th July: Open Skies

Absolutely dreadful weather. Skies have opened to torrents of rainwater, some of which leaks through our highly expensive hardwood conservatory. Garden is absolutely waterlogged, and the shed is beginning to flood. With typical foresight, realise that we both need some waterproofs and wellingtons. Am despatched to town where Milletts is busier than a discount brothel. Perhaps this is just the news that parent company Blacks Leisure needs. However, by the time I get served, there are only ladies' polka dot wellies left (puce and white). I buy a pair of these for Eunice, and a broad-brimmed rain hat for myself. The manager says she has been rushed off her feet since the end of May.

After rescuing the lawnmower and hedge trimmer from the shed, I set myself up in the den with a warming cup of cocoa and studied Blacks Leisure shares. Their results, just yesterday, showed an excellent performance. However, in spite of sliding by 200p since 2006, the shares trade at thirty-four times their 2008 forecasts. The only possibilities justifying that price, surely, are either the remote chance that Sports Direct owner Mike Ashley may make a bid, or the fear that every summer is going to be as wet as this one. Neither would encourage me to buy.

Saturday 21st July: Harry Pottering For Information

Drove Eunice into town for one of her frequent knicker-buying sprees. The woman has drawers just full of...well, drawers, but always seems to need more. She wanted to head first to Marks & Sparks, to see what Stuart Rose has to offer, and then to Bhs, once again helping enrich our man from Monte Carlo. Meanwhile, this gives me the opportunity to head off to the bookshop for a bit of further research into Amelia's whereabouts.

Arrive in the bookshop in the middle of Harry Potter mania, Piles of hardbacks of *Harry Potter and the Deathly Hallows* are stacked up, and a few furtive teenagers are leafing through to the back to see which of the key characters gets killed in the end. I finally get to speak to Ingrid Pratt, my old classmate and a friend of Amelia's, who hands over till-keeping responsibilities to a colleague for a few minutes while we talk.

"So how's Pottermania?" I ask.

"Not so good, actually," she replies.

I look around at the knots of children. "It looks really quite busy to me," I say.

"Well, it's still about the best day of the year, but that's nothing compared to what it could have been. We're selling the book at £16, which is a couple of pounds off the list price, but Tesco is selling it for a fiver. How on earth can we compete with that? They've had ninety per cent of the business."

Then I make the mistake of saying: "Well, that's free competition I suppose."

"No it's damn well not," Ingrid retorts, waving her spectacles at me. "We stock thousands of titles, pretty much as a service because most of them don't sell very well. It's damned hard work for a very meagre living as an independent, let me tell you. If it wasn't for the coffee bar we'd probably shut up tomorrow. We rely on getting good sales of blockbusters like Harry Potter to cross-subsidise the rest. Tesco sells the top 25 best-sellers and nothing else. You can't order books through them, and they have no real expertise in the field. The upshot is that by cherry-picking the big sellers, Tesco is crushing the rest of the sector. If we all go out of business, there won't be anywhere to go and browse through obscure titles and the reading public will be worse off."

After the passing of this tirade, I gradually recover from my cringe. "Anyway, I'd actually come to find out if you were still in touch with Amelia."

"Oh really?" Ingrid looked at me speculatively, sucking the end of a pencil. "Hmmm. We swapped Christmas cards until five or six years ago, but I'm sure I've got her address and phone number somewhere. I don't think she's moved." She went to her handbag, got out her address book and started to write on a Post-it.

"So Bernard, did you ever get married yourself then?"

"Oh yes. Two kids, a grandchild, the complete catastrophe."

Ingrid looked up. "And a wife?"

"Naturally," I said. "No catastrophe quite complete without one."

Ingrid continued to stare quizzically at me, one hand on her worsted hip. "Anyone I know?"

"Oh. I shouldn't think so." There was a bit of a silence.

"So at least you didn't marry that awful cow Eunice Tissington then," she said as she handed me the Post-it.

"Good grief," I laughed gamely, putting the note in my wallet. "What on earth do you take me for?"

Ingrid chuckled. "You know, I'll never forget the way she used to moon about you. And how she hated it that you were walking out with Amelia."

"Really?" I asked, genuinely curious.

"Oh God, yes. She was so catty, particularly because Amelia was so much prettier that she was. Still, that wouldn't have been hard, would it?" Ingrid roared, resting her hand on my arm. "The only things she was any good at were hockey fouls and chinese burns."

"Ah yes, chinese burns," I said lamely, recalling the time not five years ago when Eunice had twisted the skin on my arm quite expertly. She had been trying to get me to reveal where I had hidden her copy of *Fear of Flying*, whose well-thumbed pages had inspired so many of Eunice's ferocious and unprovoked hippopotamus manoeuvres.

"So are you married, then, Ingrid?" I asked, as much to derail an uncomfortable train of thought as anything.

"I was for 25 years. Bastard left me a week after my 50th birthday. It's not impossible to meet someone else when you're in your thirties, before the lines have started and your boobs don't yet point at the floor. But by forty there's grey hair, growing moles and lines to contend with. At fifty, well, it's just such a big number if you're a woman. Plus all the things that go with it: cellulite, varicose veins and bunions. It's not much of a come-on, is it?"

"Was he seeing someone else?" I found myself asking.

"Not at first. Well, unless you count bloody Charlton Athletic. Football-mad, Frank. He said I nagged. Well, you have to don't you? If you don't have any power in a relationship. A year later he's got himself a stick-thin, Thai, mail order bride of twenty-five and he's showing her off to everyone at the Coach and Horses."

"That must have been very uncomfortable."

"Well, yes, but you rise above it don't you? I've got my grandkids and my daughters, and the house of course. Anyway, on that card you'll find my number as well as Amelia's. I'd be happy to go for a quiet drink sometime, if you're interested."

Good grief. This could get complicated!

Chapter Twenty-Three

Hung Out To Dry

Monday 23rd July: Pop Idle

Bovis shares continue to fall. The idea of the bounce that I voiced last week has turned out to be nonsense. They're now down to 760p, and I'm in agonies of indecision about what to do. If I sell now, I'm merely turning a paper loss into a real one. My musings are interrupted by Eunice, who bursts into Lemon Curdistan with a copy of the *Radio Times* in hand.

"Bernard, you were watching Channel Four rubbish again after I went to bed, weren't you?"

"Er, well, not rubbish exactly."

"I seem to recall it was Nazi Pop Twins. About two racist American girl singers. Am I wrong?"

"Not sure. I think I fell asleep," I answered.

"I imagine Lord Reith would not have been impressed by your choice. Anyway, you left the TV standby button on again."

"Oh dear. How much of the Greenland ice sheet did I melt this time?" I said.

"It's not a joke, Bernard. All you have to do is get up off your corduroy posterior and turn it off at the wall. Did you know that the electricity wasted on standby buttons for electrical devices in this country would be enough to power Basingstoke?"

"I've always felt that Basingstoke would be best left in the dark where no-one could see it," I responded.

Eunice sighed and then said: "Just do it, would you?"

Tuesday 24th July: Stand By For War

Eunice, having berated me about standby buttons, has just used the washing machine to wash two mauve blouses. Nothing else in there, not even an errant sock. These two items had an hour or so to paddle about on their own at forty degrees, in a Center Parcs leisure pool for clothing, paid out of my electricity bill. Taking a deep breath, I tackle Eunice about this waste of resources.

"The colours run, you silly man," she responds. "The label says wash separately, and they're new."

I grab the Friends of the Earth checklist that Irmgard gave us and read off two figures. TV on standby uses 38 watts. Washing machine uses 2,500 watts. Perhaps, I suggest, she should shop in a more eco-friendly way before lecturing me. So rabid is the response, I am forced to lock myself in the loo for fifteen minutes.

Elevenses: Prescott, the stuffed suede pig, has suffered many indignities in his time, but last month he was given a severe mauling by Ming, Veronica's evil little pekingese. Poor creature lost a couple of handfuls of stuffing through a rip along the belly. That gave me an idea. I pulled out a little more stuffing, and created enough space for a family pack of plain chocolate McVitie's Digestives that I've been keeping as an emergency supply in the boot of the Volvo. However, found that keeping the split closed was a bit tricky until I took the ribbon off one of Jemima's teddy bears and tied it in a bow around Prescott's waist. He now sits on the floor, out of harm's way.

Thursday 26th July: Profits Of Doom

Really got out of bed the wrong side today. First, it's pouring with rain again. Second, the shed is still waterlogged and Eunice wants me to "do something". Third, and worst of all, the paper delivery boy in place of the *Telegraph* brought us a rain-sodden *Guardian*. This of course is a paper that is wet even in drought conditions. Today's scoops include tutting about how David Cameron's bicycle lights were made by Chinese mental patients, why drug addicts in Arbroath have started snorting Vim, and rejoicing in a study showing that drinking Fairtrade coffee helped single mothers in Bermondsey beat post-natal depression.

On entry to Lemon Curdistan, found the damn computer had been turned off at the wall. Thoroughly grumpy by the time it had wheezed into action and been through all its hideous routines and reminders: Your printer is short of ink, please replace the cyan immediately. You only have 968 days before your FerretForce anti-spam software expires. Upgrade now for $149.99! Update to Windows ™ GatesGalacticDomination. Click here to accept or here to wipe your hard drive.

Finally delete all these little windows, and get my share prices up by 10.30am. Markets down and falling fast. Have been trying for days to get my head round this sub-prime crisis. Being somewhat post-prime myself, understanding collateralised debt obligations, leveraged finance and other arcane lending techniques gives me a headache. All it seems to me is that vast arrays of different types of debt have been ground up into the Wall Street mincer and turned into mixed security sausage. The herbs make them smell okay, but you only need a speck of dead donkey junk bond in there to make you ill.

Wednesday 1st August: Illiquid Pub

FTSE wobbling at around 6,200. I do hope this isn't going to go on too long. I read that $43bn of loan and bond offerings have now been postponed as the debt-gobbling market finally decides it is time to go on a risk diet. If that money was going to fund private equity deals, then that's the takeover premium evaporating. I look across my portfolio and I'm not sure whether, or indeed what, to sell. Bovis is already too weak to sell, while Hornby is doing so well there seems no point. Domino's Pizza looks safe too. After all, if the City boom goes belly up, the chinless wonders may give up on champagne and truffles at the Ivy and switch to a Pepperoni Passion pizza delivered by moped.

Share club meeting at the Ring o'Bells. Cynthia and K.P. Sharma are on holiday, so the investment loonies are in charge of the asylum. Harry Staines and Martin Gale are already a little crazed after Chantelle reveals that there isn't any guest ale. Dave, the licensee, has had his credit withdrawn by the supplier. Then there's apparently a VAT 'discrepancy', which the pub's parent company is investigating. She then reveals that there are no snacks either, except chocolate covered raisins. The microwave is broken. If it means that there is no chance of a multiply reheated 'choleraburger', then we can all heave a sigh of relief.

"Presumably, that won't stop you supplying a nice fresh garden salad?" I ask in a rare moment of naivety.

"You what?" asks Chantelle, who today has yellow hair and black lipstick. "Dave's idea of a salad is two battered onion rings and a teaspoon of grated carrot with your egg and chips."

Investment discussions are rather inconclusive too. Martin Gale sees the market as a screaming buy, while I am not so sure. Chantelle, in between popping into the kitchen to make us all a round of tuna sandwiches, says we will get better prices if we wait. I can't help agreeing.

Thursday 2nd August: Women's Institute

Drive around to Dot's so that I can accompany her to the WI. There I hope to meet the investment guru who has reshaped my mother's portfolio. However, Dot is being awkward and won't get in the car.

"I can't bend down to get in there, Bernard."

"Come on, Mum, it's a Volvo, not a Trabant."

"I think me hips have packed up. I need one of those new joints like Mrs Dodd across the road got. Two weeks ago she was stiffer than Tutankhamen's teapot, but last week she was off up the Bingo like a whippet."

"Well, you've got the money, if the NHS won't do it. Smith & Nephew will see you all right either way."

"Whose nephew? Is that the nice new doctor?"

Abandoning any discussion about the manufacturers of artificial hips, I agree that we will go on foot. In Dot's case 'on foot' means driving Maurice, her mobility vehicle, repeatedly on my foot while we cross pelican crossings, awkward junctions and various other Isleworth hazards. Finally, we arrive at the hall. We're a little early and have to wait while the over-60s ladies stretch class finishes their routines. However many leg warmers, headbands and glittery leotards these hefty dames wear, they still can't fool the poor floorboards which groan like a Yorkshireman in receipt of a capital gains tax demand.

Finally the wheezing ladies depart, and we take possession of the hall. After scraping tables around, brewing obligatory cups of tea and some aimless wittering, the lady in question crystallises in the doorway. Mary Asterby is five feet of thoroughbred Surrey conservative. Suit of Thatcher blue, hair of rigid blonde and lipstick of coral. She certainly has poise and presence.

"Hello, you must be Bernard," she says holding out a ringed hand. "I've heard all about you." I rise from my seat, fighting the urge to curtsey.

"Rose?" Mary turns to an aged skinny lady in a nylon housecoat. "Have you offered Mr Jones a Peek Frean or two? Come on now, chop chop." The woman shuffles out to me with a plate of biscuits, which she offers in a palsied hand.

"I understand you helped my mother with her investments," I say to Mrs Asterby, nibbling a Bourbon. "I'm very grateful…"

"Nonsense," Mary says, briskly. "It was no trouble. However, I'm afraid we do have a bone to pick with you, Mr Jones, about the way you have been bullying your mother."

"I have not…"

"Now listen here," she says. "You have shown a distinctly over-keen interest in your mother's money. It is hers to use, abuse, spend, save or invest exactly as she sees fit. Your advice, such as it is, has been tainted with self-interest. If I were her I would cut you out of my will."

"I've done it," says Dot, smiling triumphantly. "Last week."

Aaaagghh! It can't be true, surely?

Chapter Twenty-Four

Foot And Mouth

Friday 3rd August: Bovine Bother

The market has plunged 100 points again. Thought we had a bit of a recovery. Still, I've behaved like a rabbit caught in the headlights of this liquidity crisis. I've sold nothing and bought nothing. I've got precious little fresh cash to take advantage of this weakness. If I were Martin Gale, I would raid every last bit of equity in the house, but I am naturally too cautious. If Dot really has cut me out of her will, I'll have to husband our resources carefully. It wouldn't be too bad if only Eunice would show some restraint. While I was trying to get some of my brogues out of the wardrobe today, I toppled over one of Eunice's vast shoe racks, so vast in fact it seems to have its own helipad on top. Summoned by my cursing, Eunice arrived to see me on my hands and knees burrowing through enough Cuban heels to outfit Castro's army.

"Bernard, what on earth are you doing down there?"

"I'm praying towards Mecca, what do you think?"

"Careful with the stilettos. They've only just been repaired."

"Ah yes, savaged by Ming, the wicked dogette that thinks Jimmy Choo is a command."

"Those are Clarks," Eunice said. "I wouldn't dare to dream you'd let me buy handmade shoes."

"You make up for it in quantity. I mean look at all these. Are you in training to be a bloody centipede? It would certainly explain the time it takes you to get ready. Look, where are my brogues?"

"The brown ones? I put them in the shed last month."

"What! The shed's flooded. Why did you do that?"

"Well, they're gardening shoes now aren't they?"

"I used them once when I couldn't find my wellingtons. That doesn't make them gardening shoes, does it?" I said.

"Well, they are certainly scuffed enough."

Eventually, I waded down to our personal Atlantis and saved my shoes, which are fortunately on a shelf. This is unlike the cat litter, five soaked bags of which have burst and filled the shed with a lake of fragrant spongy gruel.

6pm. Horrified to see on the news that there is a suspected bout of foot and mouth disease. Unbelievable, after the carnage of 2001. How is it we cannot seem to get this right? We don't hear about the livestock industry being decimated in the U.S. (which we read has far worse husbandry and animal health standards), nor in Europe. Yet, here we are, blighted in Blighty. I tried ringing K.P. Sharma, because I know he's got shares in cattle breeder Genus, but there's no reply and I recall he's abroad. Oh well, he'll have to take his chances.

Saturday 4th August: Credit Card Woes

Eunice's credit card bill arrives: £682.43. Clothing this month includes two pairs of shoes and two 'reversible' handbags. That's not the only reversing mishap. There's a £146.89 bill to Hide-a-Bash for the Clio, after Eunice again clipped her favourite concrete post in the Waitrose car park. My God, what's this? Ann Summers, £47.50! I don't like the sound of that at all. Hippopotamus manoeuvres are bad enough without being subjected to the indignity of edible underwear, vinyl thongs and peephole whatsits. That company must make SO much money. If only you could buy shares in it.

Elevenses: Two chocolate digestives from the stash secreted in the capacious innards of Prescott, the stuffed pig.

Sunday 5th August: Secondary Bonking Crisis

Harry Staines pops round in his battered Jaguar. While Eunice makes him some coffee, Harry whispers to me that he's got into a bit of trouble with his long-suffering wife Avril.

"Remember that sex grenade from Oxfordshire?" Harry says.

"Not rampant Delia?" I responded, warily.

"That's the one. Well, she's been writing to me again."

"Oh God. That sounds like trouble."

"She wants to see me again. I intercepted the first two letters. But Avril grabbed the third, and I got served enough tongue pie for an abattoir's summer fete. Now she's chucked me out."

"Well, you can't claim you don't deserve it," I said.

"Fair's fair, I suppose. So is it all right if I hang me hammock up here for a while?"

"Um…What about Martin? Can't he help out?" I asked. It turns out he's already stayed with Martin for a week. Chantelle refused to let him in, and Mike Delaney didn't have space.

"If you can't help me, I'll have to camp on Cynthia Valkenberg's lawn," Harry shrugs.

Finally, after consulting Eunice, it is agreed he can stay in Brian's old room. Two days only. In exchange, Harry promises to be no trouble, and to let me in on his most exciting investment.

Chapter Twenty-Five

The Toby Lifeboat

Monday 6th August: Sub-prime Toby

Daughter Jemima arrives during daylight hours for the first time in many moons. She looks haggard as she drops her bags on the floor and doesn't offer me her usual hug before heading off to the loo. Perhaps that was because Harry Staines was undressing her with his eyes from the sofa.

"For God's sake Harry," I hiss, "she's my daughter. Is there no room at all in your head for wholesome thoughts?"

I find Jem in her room, rearranging her collection of teddy bears. I go in and shut the door. "You know, Jem, I think we need to talk," I say. "You have been here for more than a year, and I really think you should offer your mother some housekeeping."

At this her lip trembles and the waterworks begin. I enfold her in my arms. My 29-year-old international lawyer daughter reverts to snivelling childhood. As always, I'm a sucker for it.

"Is it work?" I ask, gently, stroking her hair. She shakes her head, still sobbing. "It's not that git of a boss Jonathan, is it?" Another shake of the head. "You're not pregnant are you?" Another shake. "Toby?" I ask. This releases a great squall of tears.

Yes, it would be Toby. Jem's sexually ambiguous sometime boyfriend has changed orientation more often than Danny La Rue's toilet seat. Toby insists their relationship is in a 'state of reflection' at the moment, which is his customary cover for attending an Andalusian all-male wrestling pageant or a Village People tribute concert.

"Toby's got our flat on the market but the kitchen flooded last week in the deluge," Jem continued.

"On the first floor!" I spluttered. "Good grief, it seems Fulham had it worse than Tewkesbury."

"Silly, Daddy, it was a blocked gutter and the water came through the ceiling. It's not saleable, but until the kitchen's fixed we can't rent it out either. It'll have to dry out for weeks first. Toby's working crazy hours in the City and can't organise anything. He's missed four mortgage payments, and now the bank's onto us."

"I don't understand why Toby doesn't get on with direct debits," I said.

"Toby's broke, and so am I," Jem sobbed.

"How can he be? He's a derivatives dealer, isn't he?"

"Yes, but he's leveraged to the eyeballs. He's now having to buy out the other half of the place in Spain. You know, the one that he bought with Carlos."

"Ah yes, the saxophone-playing, mascara-wearing bond salesman. Why don't they just sell it?" I asked.

"Well, they're in huge negative equity after the price plunge in Spain. Besides, after they broke up Carlos fled in a queenie fit without paying any municipal bills and they stopped taking the rubbish. The place is in a huge mess."

It turns out Jem already has a personal loan of £50,000, much of which she loaned to Toby and has since disappeared, quite on what nobody knows. Then there are credit card bills. But much as my little girl wants me to, I don't have a magic wand to wave. Unfortunately, I'm not the Bank of England and cannot exercise my Greenspan put by squirting millions of pounds of fresh credit into the system. Bailing out the sub-prime Toby fund (and its apparent long-short position on heterosexuality) is considerably beyond my means. In fact, there is only person I can go to. My own mother.

Tuesday 7th August: Money On The Dot

Jem has called in sick, and I take her round to Isleworth to see Dot. My mother is pleased to see her granddaughter, and breaks out the macaroons and bakewell slices. Following my careful instructions, Jem produces an impressive tear-jerking story of riches-to-rags, replete with Tony Blair-esque hesitations in the narrative to underline the gravity of her predicament.

Dot offered her a handkerchief, and comforting words. "Look, dear. These things happen. I know, I've been through the war. We had an incendiary through the roof in Omdurman Avenue in 1940, which killed your Uncle Harold's terrapin. You can never tell when a ruddy German will hove into view and ruin everything." She levered herself out of her chair and opened her handbag.

"There," she says, handing Jem a 50p. "Here's a half crown for you. Why don't you get your Dad to buy you a lolly? That will make you feel a bit better."

It takes another hour for Jem and I to explain that what is actually required here is about £150,000, not 50p.

"Oh. I see," Dot says, finally. "Well, why not? I shan't have much use for it, will I? Best to let your family have it, I suppose, rather than hanging on until the bitter end."

Finally! The words I have waited years to hear.

Thursday 9th August: Mum And Moral Hazard

My mother is a bit like the European Central Bank. Stubborn, daft, and very rich. After barring me from my rightful inheritance for years, declaring last week she'd cut me out of her will, on Tuesday she instantly agrees to inject £150,000 of cash into that most sub-prime of all investment vehicles, a twenty-something woman. That makes the ECB's spraying around of €95 billion in inter-bank funds seem almost sensible. Jemima is earning good money in a City law firm, but has squandered it all on backless dresses, frontless shoes, and priceless hair products. She is owed £50,000 by Toby, her former boyfriend, who himself is mortgaged up to his diamanté earrings, while their jointly-owned Fulham flat lies flood-damaged and empty, its mortgage in arrears. While I would be a safe recipient of the family money, with no exposure to negative equity Marbella property, gay trysts or limited edition teddy bears, no, Dot forbids it. Only my daughter qualifies.

I can't argue that Jem doesn't need the cash, but this is moral hazard gone mad. Of course, having agreed to provide the cash, Dot and her investment svengali, Mary Asterby from the Women's Institute, will now have to take a hefty loss on many of the otherwise sensible purchases added to Dot's fund.

I am interrupted in my musings by the arrival of Eunice.

"Bernard, your harrumphing is so loud I can hear it in the bathroom. And you'll break your keyboard if you hit it so hard. Now, if you've got a minute, you did promise to adjust the feet on the Indesit. Every time it goes into the spin cycle, I swear it's about to launch itself into orbit..."

Friday 10ᵗʰ August: Obeying Hors D'oeuvres

A clutch of obscure German banks have run up big bills in risky areas, presumably knowing that their financial elders will bail them out. Now why does that sound familiar? The market is stalling, with the FTSE below 6,200, but I am dragged out of the den for matters of greater import.

Eunice has invited her awful vegan friend Irmgard and our

mentally unbalanced near-neighbour Daphne Hanson-Hart around for dinner tonight. I am tasked with making the starter, which, according to my gastroführer's mandate, is to be an organic spinach, chickpea and garlic dip. Took one look at the recipe book, an illustrated encomium written by some New Age celebrity called Hugh Funghi-Whippingboy, and decide that I shall pass over the first fourteen stages of soil kissing, spinach nurturing and chickpea soaking. While Eunice drives off to Waitrose for Irmgard's favourite Fairtrade Burundian coffee, I'm sneaking off to Tesco for a readymade starter!

Once I waltz around the hallowed aisles of our greatest retailer, I realise that here indeed is the perfect defensive stock to see us out of the current market malaise. The place is absolutely packed, and the less well-off we Britons feel, the more of us will be here looking to cut our shopping bill. In the Mediterranean food sections I find just the thing, a creamy roulade of spinach, chickpeas, tahini and garlic with just a hint of lemon, from the Finest range at £2.79. Of course, I take the opportunity to load up on some Club biscuits, a swiss roll, and a chocolate éclair from the deli. At the checkout I cover my tracks perfectly by refusing the Tesco bags, instead slipping my purchases into the Waitrose 'bag for life', a term which reminds me of my wedding vows.

However, while loading the Volvo I realise that with the wine, the own-brand single malt, the patio heater and the new foldaway gas barbecue and warming stand, I have spent £198.67. Worse still, a lot of it carries the dreaded Tesco label. Hiding this lot is going to be a problem. As I drive past the end of the road, I see Eunice, now returned and in the front garden cutting roses for the table. I drive around the block four times, but she's still there, now wittering to Daphne. Finally, I realise this idle chit-chat will never stop, and put the Volvo into the garage.

"Bernard, where on earth have you been? It's almost five."

"I realise we had run out of Fairtrade organic lemons," I say. "Can't have anything but the best, can we?"

Eunice's eyes narrow, but she returns to nattering with Daphne, while I sneak the food out of the garage back door into the kitchen. After ten minutes of frenetic ripping, I have stripped the Tesco packaging from what we will eat tonight, filled up an old cat litter sack with packets of cakes and biscuits and stashed it in the shed, and carefully placed the roulade into an earthenware dish in the fridge. The FTSE may have fallen to just over 6,000 today, but I at least have made some good, edible investments.

Chapter Twenty-Six

Sub-Prime Recipe

Saturday 11th August: Open Sesame

What a shambolic evening! Started well enough, with Eunice impressed by the neatness of my (secret Tesco) roulade and its carefully arranged lemon wedges. However, as we sat down to eat, Irmgard said to Eunice. "The dip doesn't have any sesame seeds in it, does it?"

"Well, it's Bernard's own personal creation," Eunice answered. "But I know we don't have sesame seeds in the house."

"Sorry to ask, it's just that I'm allergic."

"Oh God, that's right," said Daphne. "I remember at Doe-ra-me's christening, you went into anaphylaxis and collapsed after the finger buffet."

As all eyes swivelled to me, I tried desperately to recall the Tesco packaging, long since bagged in the recycling bin. Spinach, chickpeas, tahini, lemon juice, wasn't it? Don't recall sesame.

"You can relax, there are no sesame seeds," I said, trying to ooze the easy confidence of Jonathan Ross.

"He even went out specially to get organic Fairtrade lemons," Eunice boasted, to murmurs of approval.

"Gosh, Bernard, where did you go? Even Waitrose doesn't have those," said Irmgard.

I tapped the side of my nose, and winked. "My little secret."

"Well, Bernard, it does look scrumptious," said Daphne. "I hadn't realised you were such a dab hand in the kitchen."

It was only ten minutes after the first bite that Irmgard collapsed. A crimson rash spread all around her throat, and then as the ambulance arrived, she began a vomiting performance that would have earned her the lead role in *The Exorcist*.

7.30pm. At hospital. Irmgard on breathing machine. Have socking great bruise on my shin where Eunice kicked me after my confession, and subsequent discovery of Tesco packaging. How was I supposed to know that tahini is made of sesame seeds?

8pm. Irmgard's partner Nils arrives, pale as a ghost, with a bunch of flowers. Worried-looking doctors gather around door to intensive care. Hospital chaplain is seen hovering. Oh Lord.

12.20am. Doctors say she is past the worst, thank God. Eunice and I go home. Then begins probably the longest and most relentless harangue I have ever had the misfortune to experience. Only upside: I'll never again be asked to cook for guests.

Wednesday 15th August: Hedge Funds

Share club at the Ring o'Bells. K.P. Sharma says that today is the last day for hedge fund investors to request redemptions before the end of the third quarter. This could produce some big selling for those that allow it, and perhaps some suspensions on funds which are in difficulties. He says he has a feeling that we could get some big falls in the next day or two. I agree.

Harry Staines, now allowed back home by a very forgiving Avril, says he wants to take us out on a special investment trip. He won't let us in on what it is, but Martin, Chantelle, K.P. and I, happily pile into his old Jaguar and set off for who-knows-where. Finally, we arrive in Tunbridge Wells, and sure enough he's taking us to Ann Summers.

"No, no, Harry," complains K.P. as we stand outside the window display of PVC thigh boots and scanty underwear. "We know you can't buy shares in Ann Summers. You're wasting our time here."

"Ah," says Harry. "You can buy shares in its German equivalent, Beate Uhse. That's the European market leader. I'm only coming here to show you the kind of products and profit margins that this industry offers."

"Have you bought shares in them?" I ask.

"Yep, about three months ago. My first foray into the Jerry stock market. Did you know that the woman who started this firm was a Luftwaffe pilot and stunt woman?" Harry asked.

"Must have been to some good hen parties," Chantelle said.

With K.P refusing to go inside, me too embarrassed and Chantelle saying she's seen it all before, we go to Starbucks instead. As we sit down, K.P. brandishes his laptop, and digs up the share chart of Beate Uhse from the Internet. Then he starts to roar with laughter.

"What's so funny?" Harry asks.

"Have you made money on it yet?" K.P. asks.

"Well, no. But the market's a bit ropy at the moment."

"Just look at this." K.P. turns around the screen so we can all see the share chart for Beate Uhse AG. It looks like the trajectory of an air crash, with a plunge from 10.5 euros down to 3.5 over the last four years.

"Harry," says Chantelle, "it looks like your favourite company could do with a bit of Viagra to keep its shares up."

Chapter Twenty-Seven

Sunday Sport

Thursday 16th August: Think Tanks, No Thanks

Massive tumble overnight. Not shares, but unexpected hippopotamus manoeuvre at 5.30am. Eunice, clearly putting on weight, seems to have perforated my spleen with the buckle on her suspender belt. No sooner had I limped downstairs for breakfast and some first aid, then the FTSE showed signs of injury too. Plunged right down to 5,840! Some French bank suspended three investment funds, and there were signs of the interbank market seizing up, with overnight money rates up sharply. People are talking of a credit crunch. What should I do? Don't know. I'm like a turkey waiting for Christmas. All wattles and worry. Why can't this happen when I have spare cash to invest?

Eunice however, has it all worked out. "It's our fast-forward society," she tells me breezily over dinner. "Because of television, people aren't content to live life at its proper speed."

"For God's sake, woman, what do you know about it?" I reply, conscious we are worth several thousand pounds less now than yesterday, even if she weighs several thousand more.

"Bernard, don't be testy. Irmgard, Daphne and I were discussing it last night at baskets. Greedy people want tomorrow's consumption today, and higher interest rates are the only thing that makes them think twice."

Ah yes! Forget Davos, the OECD and the IMF. There's only one real global think tank with its finger on the pulse of the global economy, and that's the basket-weaving and macramé coven at Pit Lane Institute of Life-Long Learning. Besides, my esteemed wife is a fine one to talk about restrained consumption. She's got enough unworn comfort-fit trousers, elasticated smocks and flowery blouses to do a one-woman re-enactment of Woodstock. I'm sure she'd happily burn all her bras but for the fact that she'd never find her kneecaps again.

Friday 17ᵗʰ August: Call Waiting

Eunice is out for the evening. Jem is away on business, and I have the house to myself. After a stiff single whisky, I retrieve from the inner sanctum of my wallet the Post-It written out for me by Ingrid. Amelia's phone number and address, at least where she was until five years ago. It's forty-six years since I've seen her or heard her voice. She's now Amelia Felton, not Wrigley. I look her up on the online directory inquiries, but there is no-one of that name. Must be ex-directory, or maybe she has moved.

It's 8pm. I pick up the phone and carefully dial the number. My heart is hammering like a sixteen-year-old on a first date. An answering machine kicks in, one of those call-minder jobs: "The person you are calling is on the phone." I lose my nerve and hang up. Bloody BT, they just make it so hard. Oh God, what if it's her other half and he decides to dial 1471? I didn't withhold my number! Worse still, what if either of them dial 1471 and call back again tomorrow, and Eunice picks it up! What a total disaster that would be.

I get myself another whisky, and think. Finally I pick up the phone, dial 141 to withhold the number and then ring her again. This time a male voice answers. "Hello?"

"Sorry, is that Peking Chinese takeaway?" I ask in a moment of stir-fried inspiration.

"No, sorry." The voice sounds quite young.

"Oh, wrong number then. Sorry." I hang up and think. Could that be Amelia's son? Grandson? Toyboy? No idea. I think under the circumstances a little reconnaissance would be worthwhile. Its forty-six years after all. I don't want to rush in like a bull in a china shop.

Wednesday 22nd August: Banking On Bargains

Share club at the Ring o'Bells. K.P. Sharma has been crunching the numbers for the entire banking sector and is getting quite excited as he taps away at his laptop.

"You know, there are some seriously cheap shares out there. Look at Northern Rock! What a yield! HBOS is pretty cheap too and I like the look of Bradford & Bingley at these prices."

"Sound's good. What does everyone else think?" I say.

No-one is paying much attention. Cynthia, whose gimlet eye rarely misses a bargain, has inexplicably missed share club for several weeks now and her analysis at this point would be very welcome. Instead, we have Martin Gale trying to break his beer mat-flipping record, and Chantelle chipping away at her black nail varnish by rubbing it against her lip ring. Mike Delaney is fretting away quietly, unable to smoke and counting the minutes until it is reasonable to go out for one. Only Harry Staines, back from the bar with a pint and a paper, looks enthusiastic.

"Forget banks, chaps," he says. "How about a business whose profits are growing at 250 per cent a year, is on a price earnings ratio of 8 and pays a 10 per cent dividend?" he says.

"Great," says Martin Gale. "Is it a technology firm?"

"No, it's a piece of fiction," says K.P. Sharma. "That's just too good a combination to be true."

"Not so," says Harry, whipping out a copy of the *Sunday Sport*. "It's the owner of this esteemed organ."

"They're not doing share tips now are they?" I ask.

"Nah. It's the business itself. Generating wads of cash. Sports Media Group, is what it's called. It was formed by a reverse takeover of Sports Newspapers by Interactive World a fortnight ago. It's listed on AIM."

K.P. Sharma, head in hands, watches in despair. "Is it really that enticing, Harry?"

"Of course. It's pretty easy to make money in downmarket titles. They hardly need to recruit any big name journalists, and they can charge a fortune for the adult advertising. With plans for a circulation push they'll get economies of scale."

I pick up the rag gingerly. "This is just offensive rubbish," I say. There, lurking between the full colour pictures of scantily-clad women, are stories about a liberal front bench spokesman snapped with a stripper astride him in a lap dancing club (headlined 'Lib-lap packed'), a call-girl's claim that Pavarotti died in her bed ('Pav's lust cost us a tenor') and so on.

"What's your take on the quality of management?" K.P. asks Harry. "Do they have flair, vision and integrity?"

"Who ever knows?" Harry retorts. "At least expectations won't be too high. That might make it a bit different from any of those banks should they end up having some dodgy loans."

In the end we vote against Harry's suggestion, and instead buy 200 Northern Rock at 718p, which we all agree is not a bad price at all, saving a fiver against the year's high.

Chapter Twenty-Eight

Cynthia Shackled

Wednesday 5th September: The Resurgent Loonie

Share club at Ring o'Bells. K.P. Sharma is just telling us how he bought some shares in Land Securities at the bargain price of £15.75, when Cynthia Valkenberg walks in, looking a little unwell.

"Where on earth have you been?" K.P. asks. "No phone calls returned, no e-mails. We've been unable to make decisions on the share club portfolio. We've missed lots of bargains."

"Well, I guess you'll have to forgive me," she says. "I went back to Canada to see some associates who are setting up a currency hedge fund and made the mistake of flying to New York for a couple of days to see a potential backer. The Feds were waiting for me at JFK with a warrant."

"Good grief," said Martin Gale. "Surely it was a mistake?"

"No mistake, I'm afraid. I was a non-executive director of an Antiguan-based blackjack website for five months. It doesn't matter that the venture folded way back in 2003, I'm still in danger under the Federal Wire Act for bets transmitted between players in the U.S. and the remote servers. So the upshot is that I'm only here for a week or two to arrange further collateral for the surety put up by one of my associates. I'll have to sell my investments, and maybe my home too. The lawyers are probably going to get most of it."

"How awful for you," I say, and offer to buy her a drink. She fills us in on the awful details the misery of the holding cells and of doing the 'perp walk' the manacled shuffle for attendant photographers that is an important part of U.S. judicial humiliation.

"It's a real shame," she says. "No least because I've got some great positions in the loonie and I'll have to close them."

Even Harry is waiting for the punchline on this one. She explains that the loonie is the Canadian dollar, and it looks set to make parity with the U.S. dollar for the first time since 1976. She and K.P. go into a huddle, deciding how to liquidate her entire investment without damaging the share club's portfolio too much.

Thursday 6ᵗʰ September: Purse And Perception

Eunice has gone to the video shop, but rings me from the store to say she has left her purse behind in the kitchen and would I be good enough to read out the card number. I take the cordless phone into the kitchen. Sure enough the purse is on the work surface, though 'purse' is hardly the word. It's more the scale of a villain's holdall, with brass rivets and room for jemmy and sawn-off shotgun. How can you call this object, the same size as a recently slaughtered piglet, a purse? It's like calling a camper van a moped.

"Come on Bernard, there's a queue," Eunice says.

"I'm looking. It isn't with the other cards."

"Yes it IS."

"Well, there's the M&S card, the Debenhams card, the Ann Summer's bulk-purchasers discount…"

"Bernard, will you stop that and find it!"

I decide to tip the whole thing out, which sends a cascade of coins, keys, boiled sweets, receipts and old tube tickets out onto the counter. Among the coins are a dozen pfennigs (of all useless things), a two euro coin, some Irish pennies, a ripped corner of a ten pound note, a leaking AAA battery, several safety pins and a Glyndebourne ticket from 1989. There is also an ancient collar and bell which belonged to our previous cat, Swot.

"I'm sorry it's really not here, Eunice," I say.

"It IS there. It's between my Lloyds TSB cashcard and the WI membership card."

Finally I do find it and read out the number. From the haranguing I get afterwards, I can tell that my eventual success has not softened Eunice's temper.

Saturday 8th September: High Tea Is The Future

My mother is over for tea, with Brian, Janet and the Antichrist, plus Jem. After tucking into a slice of fruitcake, Dot says: "I remember the Lyons' corner houses, you know. Most cafés and wotsits have shut down now, haven't they?"

We all nod at the truth of this remark.

"Still," she says brightly. "It's the future again now isn't it? All the young people are getting qualifications and going into computerised catering with cake and scones and everything."

While Dot turns to take another slice, I catch the Antichrist circling his finger at his head and crossing his eyes. He's right, she has got a screw loose, but I clip his ear anyway.

"What do you mean, Mum?"

"Well, Mrs Davies's son, he's got a PhD and he's going in for it. So are Mr Potter's boys, and they've both been to University."

"Going in for what though?"

"They're both something in high tea. That's what they say."

Chapter Twenty-Nine

Destiny With Pears

Monday 10th September: Amelia Visit

Up early and with a purpose. I'm definitely going to see Amelia today. Eunice caught me whistling to myself in the bathroom mirror, and marched up to find out what was the matter.

"It's a morning, Bernard. You're grumpy in the mornings. Don't you remember?" Eunice proclaimed loudly. Her proximity forced me into a rather too vigorous stroke with the Gillette Fusion. It left five neat parallel cuts across my neck, rather like miniature shark gills. Damn! Damn! Today of all days.

"Now look what you've made me do," I said testily.

"Aha, that's better. Normal Bernard service resumed," announced Eunice cheerily. "Now, as you may recall, I shall be going with Irmgard and Daphne to the macramé outing today."

"Yes, I know. You're all off to get knotted."

"Ha-ha. Very droll. Now Dolores Smedley is going to give us a lift..."

"Ah, Dolores, the Bottle Beast of Chislehurst. Is she still on two bottles of Crème de Menthe a day?" I asked.

"No, she never touches a drop, which is why she's driving," Eunice said crisply.

"So where is it that you are all going?"

"Oh Bernard, please. I explained all this yesterday, don't you listen? We're going to the exhibition at the South Bank and then after lunch going on the London Eye and then perhaps see a film."

Witches of Eastbourne, I imagine. Hmm.

I waited for Eunice to depart and then assembled my supplies: Spare plasters in case my neck started bleeding again, a thermos flask of coffee, sunglasses, three copies of *Chronic Investor* (perhaps with extended surveillance a chance to try to get my head around that 'structured investment products' masterclass), a packet of jaffa cakes and of course the obligatory mackintosh without which no stake out is complete. With my copy of Nicholson's *Streetfinder* paper-clipped open to page 104, I drove off to Orpington.

Traffic was, as usual, horrendous, and I missed my turning off Farnborough Way towards Orpington Hospital. Doing a hurried three-point turn on the forecourt of a filling station I managed to scrape the back of the Volvo on a hitherto invisible concrete post, just nine inches high. These blasted things, camouflaged in the same beige concrete that disfigures most of urban Britain, manage to leap out from every kind of hiding place to assail the unwary: the corners of busy junctions, garden centre loading bays, supermarket car parks and even private drives. They must be the best-performing portfolio of assets that the British car repair industry has ever had. Eunice, who admittedly drives by Braille, has managed to run up more than twelve hundred quid's worth of scratches, bumps and dents in less than eighteen months, not one of them worth claiming on insurance for because of the vast excess we are forced into these days.

So in a scraped car, with a scratched neck and a less than perfect temper I find my way up towards Orpington Hospital and make the required clutch of left and right turns to bring me to a halt opposite number fourteen Antrobus Crescent. The house is a classic 1930s semi-detached mock Tudor affair with a neatly kept garden and a Citroen Saxo in the drive. There is no-one to be seen, and I settle down for my first chocolate covered treat. It is perhaps only ten minutes later when I notice that the tree visible over the garage is no ordinary suburban ash or sycamore. My binoculars confirm what I first thought; that it is a pear tree, heavy with fruit. This, surely, can be no coincidence. This is the Amelia Wrigley for whom in May 1961, I carved "BJ loves AW" on a pear tree in the orchard at Old Dorringsfield, and who a mere fortnight or so later deflowered me, gloriously and unexpectedly, on Ascension night. Then she let me have the cataclysmic news that her family was emigrating the very next day to Australia, a development I had known nothing about and which, as she told me, she had thought would never come to pass.

As I watch, I see some movement behind the large vertical stained glass window, which lights the staircase, and the front door opens. A dark-haired petite woman, wearing a charming straw sunhat and carrying a gardener's kneeler and a pair of secateurs, makes her way across the lawn and disappears from view behind some bushes. I couldn't see her face, but the hammering in my heart confirms my suspicions. It must be her. The sun is now shining, and a bird is singing lyrically in some high tree. Really, it is now or never.

I look in the mirror, grinning toothily to see if I have any jaffa cake remains between my teeth, then comb what remains of my hair. The plaster on my neck is a bit of a disaster and I grimace as I rip it off. It's agony, but fortunately, the bleeding doesn't re-start. The tie was perhaps a bit formal, but I leave it on anyway as it goes well with the jacket. Opening the door, I lever myself out and head towards the gate. I lean over, fiddling with what is actually a very simple catch, when she looks up at me. Her face is soft and warm, the blue eyes undimmed. That disarming smile is still framed by lovely dimples.

"I'm sorry. We're C of E," she says.

"Um, pardon?." This has thrown me completely.

"If that is *Watchtower* or *Awake* I'm afraid you're wasting your time," she says standing up and pointing her secateurs at the copy of *Chronic Investor* I find I still have in my hand. "Because…"

She stops for a moment, her mouth open.

"No, it's not that," I say. "I just came to see you again…Amelia. It's me…"

"Oh. Bernard, it is you, isn't it?"

"Yes. I've…"

"It is *really* you. My goodness. You are looking well, really well. Apart from the shaving of course."

"So are you, you look so…unchanged." And happy, I suppose. Should I rejoice in that?

"Well, don't just stand there, Bernard, come on in. I'm sure you could do with a cup of tea. Or perhaps a cold drink?"

In a moment I was sitting in Amelia's kitchen drinking tea, taking in the deeply-scored breadboard, the chipped teapot, the Tefal breadmaker and the LG microwave. I could hardly bear to look at her face, in all its luminous intensity, because of the feelings it provoked. I was so close to tears, balanced between joy and sadness. There were lines, yes, and some grey hair. Much less than I'd expected. The laughter and the cheeky grin were somehow the same.

For two hours we talked about her kids (two sons) and mine, her grandkids (a daughter and a son) and mine. The house she had inherited when her parents died in the 1980s, and which she had moved back into, with family in tow. We did all the easy stuff. We looked at our wedding rings, and didn't speak about our ties to others. I mentioned the pear tree, and yes, she had planted it thinking of me. She took me out into the back garden and showed me the tree. Sunlight filtered through the branches, dappling us both. Amelia looked up at me, and I realised that we had boarded a runaway emotional express.

"Would you like to go for a walk?" I asked, as we returned to the house.

"Maybe," she said. "But I've got a better idea." She checked the kitchen clock and nodded to herself, then led me up the staircase, past framed photographs of her wedding day, her baby sons, and various anniversaries.

"I think we should use the spare room, don't you?" she said. My dry throat refused a response. She opened a door into a bedroom which was spread with sewing materials, and a host of rather elderly toys. She closed the curtains, which bathed the room in a rosy glow, and took me in her arms. The kiss was slow, soft and passionate. I felt my toes tingle.

"You know, Bernard, I would never have dared to do this when I was twenty, or thirty or perhaps even at forty," she said. "It takes getting to our age to be able to know that we have earned the right to a final taste of each other."

She took off her clothes and mine, and slowly caressed me as she had all those years ago. Then she guided me into her, where instinct took over and all the heavy lost decades evaporated like dew. Afterwards, with the curtains parted and a lowering sun gilding our still-heaving bodies I was sure I could smell the scent of pears.

"You've got to go home now," she said. "You do understand, don't you? It's nearly five."

"Of course. It's been wonderful, Amelia, really wonderful. I needed to know about us, that's all."

"So did I. But now we have to put a frame around this lovely afternoon and leave it as a treasured memory, in a drawer somewhere. I'll always love you. I always did, but we've got different lives to live now."

In the car, on the way home, I stopped off at the orchard in Old Dorringsfield. The Celandine Homes sign is still there, but most of the builders' materials have gone and the fence has been trampled down. The stumps of the Worcester Pearmain trees are getting old and darkened now, but right in the middle there is one fresh, raw stump. The pear tree I had tried to save is gone, proof of the vindictiveness of the Harmsworth brothers. But now, for some reason, I don't seem to mind as much.